Fondue and Casserole Cookery

Other Concorde Books

MRS BEETON'S FAVOURITE RECIPES

MRS BEETON'S FAVOURITE CAKES AND BREADS

MRS BEETON'S PARTY DISHES

MRS BEETON'S SWEET DISHES

GARDENING FOR BEGINNERS

MAKING AND PLANNING A SMALL GARDEN

SIMPLE GREENHOUSE GARDENING

SIMPLE VEGETABLE GROWING

COLLECTING ANTIQUE SILVER

COLLECTING ENGLISH ANTIQUES

Cover picture: Fondue Bourgignonne (by courtesy of Tabasco Pepper Sauce)

Frontispiece: Cheese Fondue (by courtesy of the Swiss Cheese Union)

Fondue and Casserole Cookery

Edited by
Maggie Black

Concorde Books

WARD LOCK LIMITED · LONDON

ACKNOWLEDGEMENTS

The compiler and editor would like to thank all the people and the institutions and manufacturers, who have supplied specialist advice, photographs and new material.

Particular thanks are due to Tabasco Pepper Sauce for the specially-taken cover photograph.

The following also deserve special thanks: the Swiss Cheese Union (for the frontispiece); the Fruit Producers' Council (for a considerable number of specially-taken and other colour photographs), the Kellogg Company of Great Britain, the Oxo Meat Cookery Service, Taunton Cider Ltd., the Dutch Dairy Bureau.

ISBN cased edition 0 7063 15405
ISBN paper edition 0 7063 15413

First published in Great Britain 1973 by Ward Lock Limited, 116 Baker Street, London, W1M2BB

Designed by Andrew Vargo

Text in Baskerville (169/312)

Set and printed Offset Litho in England by Cox & Wyman Ltd., London, Fakenham and Reading

Contents

Weights and Measures Used in this Book

Liquid measures

60 drops	1 teaspoon
3 teaspoons	1 tablespoon
4 tablespoons	$\frac{1}{2}$ gill
1 gill	$\frac{1}{4}$ pint
4 gills	1 pint
2 pints	1 quart
4 quarts	1 gallon

Homely solid measures

Spoons are British Standard teaspoons and tablespoons, which hold the amounts of liquid given above. They are measured with the contents levelled off, i.e. all the spoonfuls are level spoonfuls.

The cup is a British Standard measuring cup which holds 10 fluid oz or an Imperial $\frac{1}{2}$ pint.

Homely solid measures

Flour, sifted	3 tablespoons	1 oz
Castor or granulated sugar	2 tablespoons	$1\frac{1}{4}$ oz
Icing sugar, sifted	3 tablespoons	1 oz
Butter or margarine	2 tablespoons	$1\frac{1}{4}$ oz
Cornflour	2 tablespoons	1 oz
Granulated or powdered gelatine	4 teaspoons	$\frac{1}{2}$ oz
Golden syrup or treacle	1 tablespoon	1 oz
Flour, sifted	1 cup	5 oz
Castor or granulated sugar	1 cup	9 oz
Icing sugar, sifted	1 cup	5 oz
Butter or margarine	1 cup	9 oz
Cornflour	1 cup	8 oz
Golden syrup or treacle	1 cup	1 lb

Metric measures

Precise metric equivalents are not very useful. The weights are almost impossible to measure accurately, and are not used in ordinary cooking.

Schools use a 25-gram unit for 1 oz and for re-tested recipes. This means that they can use existing equipment. For instance, a 6-inch sandwich tin can be used for a 15-cm one, and a 7-inch tin for an 18-cm one. Yorkshire pudding using 100 grams plain flour fits into a 2×14 cm (8 in $\times 5\frac{1}{2}$ in) baking tin.

Mrs Beeton's recipes are all being re-tested so that they can be converted to metric measures when these come into general use.

Introduction

FONDUES AND CASSEROLES deserve a book to themselves if only because they are ideal dishes for parties.

For any number up to ten, what could be better than an informal, friendly group round a chafing or fondue dish, stretching to dip their bread, meat or rolled 'bite' in the steaming sauce or oil? The 'fondue' atmosphere makes for goodwill and relaxed enjoyment.

A relaxed hostess too, since everything is done beforehand except the actual cooking process—and since that takes place at the table, she has no work in the kitchen just before her guests arrive! She has only to dress herself, and set *them* to work.

She is helped, of course, by the fact that any fondue is a full-bodied meal. She need only serve a salad with it or before it, and fresh fruit or the simplest fruit dish afterwards.

It's difficult to crowd more than ten people round a fondue dish, though, without risk of accidents. Besides, a real fondue dish only holds enough sauce for this number. If you try to make a larger fondue, it is almost impossible to keep the whole dish at the right temperature. So for a crowd—any number over ten—easy-care casseroles are the obvious answer instead. Our selection for you ranges from the great classics to many kinds of casseroles—even sweet ones—from home and abroad, which all make first-class dishes for a big party.

All these dishes freeze well, either before or after cooking. So you can make two batches when preparing for a party, cutting costs by buying in bulk, and effort by only doing one lot of cutting-up and washing-up. This way, you can always be equipped to give an unexpected party at a moment's notice.

Again there is no work just beforehand for the cook-hostess since these dishes either look after themselves or welcome reheating. Long-cooking 'bakes', which Americans have made an art of their own, are included. So are various toppings to change a dish's looks and flavour, and salads to go with one and all. Breads, too, and some super garnishes!

Finally, just to make the hostess's life even easier, we give you some menus for whole casserole-baked meals.

These features make fondues and casseroles particularly good party fare for 'teenagers' and other young people's parties. They're popular too.

But of course they are fine for ordinary family meals as well. Especially for winter evenings! The working housewife will find them a boon, easily prepared ahead, always good-tempered, and mostly cheap to make. Economy cooking really is possible when you 'go for' fondues and casseroles because so many bits and pieces can be used up in savoury, useful ways, and most of the main ingredients are usually cheap too—although a drop of Cognac or a little wine is a wonderful luxury addition to many of them.

As a final bonus, there's the pleasant fact that, today, gay, appealing, yet sturdy, decorated fondue dishes and casseroles are more widely available than ever before. So the housewife who decides to 'feature' these dishes can have a wonderful time making her choice from the varied materials and styles on display.

The Editor

Cheese Fondues

CLASSIC CHEESE FONDUE

10–14 oz Emmentaler cheese	**1 heaped teasp cornflour** *or* **potato flour**
10–14 oz Gruyère cheese	**1 liqueur glass kirsch**
1 clove garlic	**Pepper, nutmeg** *or* **paprika to taste**
4 glasses white wine	
2–4 teasp lemon juice	

Rub round the inside of an earthenware casserole with garlic and warm up the wine together with the lemon juice. Add the cheese gradually, stirring all the time. Boil up on a good heat, then add the kirsch mixed to a smooth paste with the cornflour. Continue to cook for a short time, stirring the fondue all the time in the form of the figure '8', with a whisk. Stand the fondue on a spirit-stove which can be regulated, so that it continues to boil very slowly. Each person serves himself from the casserole. The creamy cheese mixture is eaten by spearing a cube of bread on a fork, stirring it in the mixture several times and then transferring the cube to the mouth.

If you have no kirsch at hand, try 'Round the World' fondues by substituting Cognac, gin, whisky or sherry for the kirsch; or exchange the white wine for half the quantity of dry vermouth, or the full quantity of cider or a rosé wine. The fondue will, of course, have a different taste, but it will be very good.

Why not try varied breads too? For example, granarye or whole wheat bread cubes can be delicious.

4 helpings

CHEESE FONDUE WITH BREAD STICKS

1 oz butter	**Seasoning**
1 oz flour	**Ready-made French mustard**
½ pt milk	
½ lb Gruyère cheese, grated	

Melt the butter over very gentle heat. Add the flour, and cook together very gently for 3–4 min. Add the milk gradually, stirring without ceasing. Mix the cheese and seasonings, and add them slowly to the sauce. Heat, stirring, but do not allow to reach boiling point. Serve in the cooking dish, standing over a low heat. Use the following bread sticks to dip into the fondue.

Bread Sticks (*Method, p. 12*)

1 lb flour	**1 teasp sugar**
½ teasp salt	**Warm water**
½ oz yeast	

Dutch Fondue

the liquid to the boil in the fondue pan. Lower the heat, and stir in the cheese and flour by spoonfuls, stirring continuously. When melted add the Calvados and season to taste.

To serve, dip the apple cubes in the fondue instead of bread or with it.

6 helpings

Sift the flour into a warm bowl with the salt and stand in a warm place. Cream the yeast with the sugar and add this, with warm water, to the flour to form a pliable dough. Knead well with a floured hand and return to the clean warm bowl. Cover with a cloth and stand in a warm place 1 hr to rise. Turn on to a floured board and knead again. Cut off 1-oz portions and knead and roll these into long sticks or pencil shapes 3–4 in long. Place on a greased and floured baking tray and allow to rise ½ hr in a warm place. Bake at the top of a hot oven, 230 °C, 450 °F., Gas 8, for 10–15 min until brown and crisp.

Cool on a rack and use immediately they are cool.

CIDER FONDUE

1½ lb grated Gruyère and Emmentaler cheese, mixed	Salt and freshly ground black pepper to taste
2 tablesp flour	6–8 crisp red eating apples, cored and cubed, dipped in lemon juice
¾ pt dry still cider	
1 teasp dry mustard	
3 tablesp Calvados	

Dredge the cheese with the flour. Blend a little of the cider with the mustard, then blend this into the remaining cider. Bring

DUTCH FONDUE

20 oz Edam cheese, coarsely grated	White ground pepper
6 eggs	Chopped parsley
1 oz butter	Fingers of dry hot toast
½ teasp cornflour	
Milk	

Put the cheese into a bowl, just cover with milk and leave overnight, or for 8 hr.

To cook, pour the cheese and milk into the top of a double boiler with simmering water below. Beat the eggs until liquid. Blend the cornflour with the butter, and add to the cheese, then stir in the eggs. Cook very gently, stirring constantly, until the mixture is melted and smooth.

Pour immediately into deep soup plates or bowls, sprinkle with a few grains of pepper and the chopped parsley. Serve with the finger of toast.

6 helpings

ENGLISH APPLE FONDUE

¾ pt pure apple juice	¼ level teasp paprika
1 clove garlic	1½ lb English Cheddar cheese coarsely grated
1 level tablesp cornflour	
¼ level teasp dry English mustard	

Choose a pan big enough to take the juice. Rub the inside with the cut clove of garlic. Blend the cornflour, mustard and paprika, and mix to a paste with a little apple

English Apple Fondue ▶

juice. Warm the remaining juice in the casserole, add the cheese gradually, and stir until melted. Stir in the cornflour paste, bring to simmering point, and simmer for 10–15 min until creamy, stirring continuously.

Serve with cut chunks of fresh eating apple dipped in lemon juice, and with French bread or crisp, hot toast.

6 helpings

CHEESE AND TOMATO FONDUE

2 lb tomatoes	1 teasp powdered
1 tablesp	basil
cornflour	Salt and freshly
¼ pt rosé wine	ground black
¾ lb Gruyère and	pepper to taste
Emmentaler	French bread
cheese, mixed	cubes

Drop the tomatoes into boiling water, drain and skin. Simmer in ¾ pt water until pulpy, then strain through a sieve. Keep both the liquid and the purée. Bring the purée to the boil in the fondue pan. Blend the cornflour with a little of the wine, then add the remaining wine to it. Add this gradually to the purée. Cook for 3–4 min, stirring, then gradually add the cheese mixed with the basil. Serve when the cheese has melted, by dipping the bread cubes in the mixture.

8 helpings

PARMESAN FONDUE FOR TWO

3 eggs	Salt
4 oz Parmesan	A little cayenne
cheese, grated	pepper
2 oz butter,	
unsalted	

Beat the eggs until liquid, then gradually add the rest of the ingredients, mixing well. Place in a fondue pan over moderate heat, and stir briskly until the mixture resembles thick cream. Serve immediately.

For a milder fondue, use 2 oz grated Parmesan cheese and 2 oz grated Emmentaler cheese.

2 helpings

TOMATO FONDUE

¾ lb mature	¼ pt condensed
Cheddar cheese,	tomato soup
coarsely grated	from can
¼ lb blue cheese,	2 tablesp sherry
crumbled	
1 teasp Worcester	
sauce	

Mix the cheeses, sauce and soup in the fondue pan. Stir briskly over a very low heat until the cheeses melt. Add the sherry just before serving. Do not allow to boil. Serve with chunks of wholewheat or granarye bread.

4 helpings

Meat Fondues

MEAT (AND SEAFOOD) FONDUES can be served informally, or for a sophisticated occasion.

As for a cheese fondue, the guests or family sit round the table as the cooking takes place there. But this time each person has a plateful of tender meat cubes, prawns or other seafood. He spears his bite-sized piece, cooks it in sizzling oil in a central pot, and then dips it in one of a selection of savoury dips and sauces on the table before eating it.

Strangers to the game should be warned that the fork and the meat are *hot*. Plenty of paper napkins should be provided, and possibly a second fork for each diner.

A deeper pot than a fondue dish is also needed, one which is narrow at the top and wider based, to prevent the oil from spattering.

If more than four people take part, there should be two pots of oil at least.

FONDUE BOURGIGNONNE (Shown on front cover)

Allow 6–8 oz fillet or similar lean beef per person. Remove any sinews and fat, and cut into bite-sized cubes (1-in pieces).

Put enough cooking oil into a suitable flameproof pot to fill it nearly $\frac{1}{2}$ full. Heat the oil on the stove until very hot–375°, if using a sugar thermometer, or until a cube of bread browns in less than a minute. Transfer immediately to the fondue stand, and keep at a regular heat by adjusting the flame underneath.

Each person spears a cube of meat on a fork, and places it in the hot oil. The meat only takes a few moments to cook, the exact time depending on the preference of the individual. The meat is then seasoned with one of the sauces below, and is transferred to another fork for eating. One should not attempt to eat the meat from the fondue fork, as this gets very hot and can burn the mouth.

Savoury Sauce

Scant $\frac{1}{4}$ pt mayonnaise	$\frac{1}{2}$ teasp Tabasco Sauce
2 dessertsp finely-chopped onion	1 teasp vinegar (mild)
2 finely-chopped gherkins	Salt and castor sugar to taste
3–4 dessertsp tomato sauce	

Mix the mayonnaise with the tomato sauce, Tabasco Sauce and vinegar. Stir in the chopped onion and gherkins, and add salt and sugar to taste.

Barbecue Sauce

1 medium onion, finely diced	$\frac{1}{4}$ teasp Worcester Sauce
5 tablesp tomato ketchup	1 teasp salt
4 tablesp olive oil	Juice of $\frac{1}{2}$ lemon
$1\frac{1}{2}$ gills water	1 tablesp wine vinegar
2 oz Demerara sugar	1 teasp Tabasco Sauce

In a frying pan, sauté the onion in 1 tablesp oil until transparent. Mix together the remaining ingredients and add to the onion. Cook over a low flame for 20 min to reduce.

Mushroom-Sour Cream Sauce

1 oz butter	$\frac{1}{2}$ pt soured cream
1 onion, finely chopped	Salt and pepper
4 oz mushrooms, finely chopped	$\frac{1}{4}$ teasp Tabasco Sauce
1 tablesp parsley, finely chopped	

Melt the butter in the pan. Add the onion and mushrooms, and cook gently until tender but not brown. Drain well. Add onion, mushrooms and parsley to the soured cream. Stir in the seasoning and Tabasco Sauce, and mix all well together. If the sauce is too thick, add a little milk. Serve cold.

Diable Sauce

1 tablesp chopped onion	$\frac{1}{2}$ bay leaf
	6–8 peppercorns, crushed
1 oz butter	8–10 drops Tabasco Sauce
1 level tablesp flour	
$\frac{1}{2}$ pt good brown stock	$\frac{1}{2}$ teasp English mustard, made up
1 tablesp vinegar	

Cook the onion in the butter until soft and transparent. Add the flour, and cook for a few minutes. Add the stock and vinegar and stir until boiling. Add bay leaf and peppercorns, and simmer for 10 min. Strain, then add the Tabasco Sauce and mustard.

CHICKEN LIVER FONDUE

$1\frac{1}{2}$ lb chicken livers	$\frac{1}{4}$ teasp pepper
	$\frac{1}{2}$ teasp oregano
$1\frac{1}{2}$ gills salad or peanut oil	Béchamel sauce, mushroom sauce,
2 cloves garlic, pounded or crushed	onion sauce, cider sauce, savoury orange sauce
2 tablesp white wine vinegar	

Cut the chicken livers into bite-sized chunks. Marinate in the oil, garlic, vinegar and seasonings for 1–2 hr. Drain well, and pat dry. Serve with some or all of the sauces suggested.

FRANKFURTER FONDUE

1 lb frankfurters	1 tablesp onion, finely chopped
1 lb Gruyère cheese, coarsely grated	1 teasp dry English mustard
2 tablesp flour	
1 clove garlic, pounded	Salt and freshly ground black pepper to taste
2 cups dry white wine	3 tablesp brandy

Simmer the frankfurters in water for about 10 min, until tender. Cut them into bite-sized pieces. Dredge the cheese with the flour. Put the garlic and wine into the fondue pan (use a cheese fondue dish for this fondue) and heat until bubbling. Gradually stir in the cheese, onion and mustard, stirring without ceasing. When the cheese has melted, season to taste and add the brandy. Serve very hot, and use the frankfurter chunks for dipping into the sauce.

FRIED SWEETBREAD FONDUE

1½ lb lambs' sweetbreads	Butter or good dripping
Seasoned flour	
Egg and breadcrumbs, to coat	

Wash and soak the sweetbreads under dripping cold water for 1–2 hr until free from blood. Cut off any skin, gristle and ragged ends. Put into a saucepan, cover gently with fresh cold water, and bring slowly to the boil. Drain. Press between two plates until cold and firm. Cut into bite-sized pieces. Roll in the seasoned flour, and coat with the egg and breadcrumbs. Fry briefly in the hot fat. Serve on paper napkins with fondue forks, and offer savoury lemon or orange sauce, and one or two sauces made with white wine.

6 helpings

HAM OR BACON FONDUE (hot or cold)

1¼ lb boiled ham or bacon cut in ¾-in cubes	For a cold fondue Sauces as below Green salad
For a hot fondue:	
Flour	
Beaten egg	
Brown breadcrumbs	
Sauces as below	

For a hot fondue, heat oil, in a meat fondue pot. Prepare the meat cubes by tossing in flour, and then coating with the egg and breadcrumbs. Allow to firm up,

by standing, before use. When dipped into the hot oil, they will crisp in seconds, being ready-cooked.

Suitable sauces include:
Cider Sauce, Cumberland Sauce, Agro-Dolce, Savoury Orange Sauce, Sour-Sweet Sauce.

For a cold fondue for summer use, the meat need not be coated. The cubes can be speared on cocktail sticks, and dipped in one of the following:
Creamed Yogurt Dip, Curried Cream-Cheese Dip, Savoury Sauce, Mushroom-Sour Cream Sauce.

Serve with pumpernickel and a green salad.

This fondue makes an excellent dish for a summer lunch out of doors, or for a picnic. The dips and sauces can be carried in closed cartons.

4 helpings

KIDNEY FONDUE

Lambs' or veal kidneys	Sauces of your choice
Flour	

Skin the kidneys and wipe them. Split them open and remove the cores, then cut them into quarters or bite-sized pieces (if using veal kidneys). Dredge lightly with flour before putting the kidney pieces on the guests' plates.

Serve with any of the sauces suggested for Fondue Bourguignonne, or with Espagnole, Italian or mushroom sauce.

LAMB FONDUE

1¼ lb lean lamb, cut from leg	Sauces as below

Cut the meat into neat ¾-in cubes. Heat the oil in the meat fondue pot, and divide the meat cubes among the diners. Serve with some or all of the following sauces:
Savoury Lemon Sauce, Onion Sauce, Reform Sauce, Soubise Sauce, Tomato Sauce.

PORK OR VEAL FONDUE

2 lb lean pork or veal, cut in 1-in cubes　　**Sauces of your choice**

Put ½ lb cubes on each of 4 plates. As usual, the diners spear and cook their own meat, and dip it in the sauce they prefer.

Suitable sauces for these fondues would be:
Savoury Lemon Sauce, Onion Sauce, Savoury Sauce, Mushroom-Sour Cream Sauce.

4 helpings

The top-quality meat needed for frying in a fondue can be expensive. For an economy dish, try the following meat balls or croquettes.

MEAT BALLS

1 small onion　　**1½ teasp salt**
A little lard　　**¼ teasp white pepper**
4 oz raw beef
2½ oz pork　　**1 teasp sugar**
1–1½ cups milk　　**1–2 tablesp butter**
1 egg　　　　*or* **cream**
2 tablesp breadcrumbs　　**(optional)**
1 teasp potato flour

Peel, slice and fry onions slightly in a little lard. Wash meat and pass 3 times through mincer, together with the fried onion or blend in an electric blender for a few seconds. Mix milk and egg; soak breadcrumbs and flour in this, add salt, pepper, sugar, cream or butter (if used) and finally the meat. Mix well. Make into small balls and fry brown in oil.

Meat balls are a favourite dish in Sweden and can be eaten fried or boiled with potato salad with various sauces such as Creole Sauce, Mushroom Sauce, Piquant or Tomato Sauce.

4 helpings

SAUSAGE MEAT BALLS OR CAKES

1 lb pork　　**6 sage leaves (optional)**
1 lb lean veal
1 lb beef suet　　**1–8 teasp marjoram (optional)**
½ lb breadcrumbs
Grated rind of ½ lemon　　**¼ teasp savoury herbs (optional)**
1–8 teasp grated nutmeg　　**Sausage skins**
Salt and pepper

Remove all the skin and gristle from the pork. Chop or mince the pork, veal and suet together very finely. Add the breadcrumbs, lemon rind, nutmeg, seasoning and the herbs if desired, which must all be very finely chopped. Mix together very thoroughly. Form the mixture into balls or meat cakes, flour and fry them.

Serve to the diners ready fried, with some or all of the following sauces:
Cider Sauce, Curry Sauce, Devil Sauce, Piquant Sauce.

CHICKEN CROQUETTES

8 oz cold chicken *or* fowl (boned)　　**2 oz cooked ham *or* tongue**
1 truffle (optional)　　**1 oz butter**
1 tablesp cream *or* milk　　**1 oz flour**
1 teasp lemon juice　　**¼ pt stock**
Salt and pepper　　**Egg and fresh breadcrumbs**
6 button mushrooms

Chop the chicken and ham or tongue finely. Melt the butter in a saucepan, stir in flour, stir in stock slowly, boil 3–5 min. Add all other ingredients, chopping the mushrooms and truffle, turn on to a plate to cool. Form into cork-shapes, coat with egg and fresh breadcrumbs, fry until golden brown in hot, deep fat. Drain. Serve with some or all of the following sauces:
Creole Sauce, Curry Sauce, Devil Sauce, Diable Sauce, Onion Sauce, Tomato Sauce.

Seafood Fondues and Chowders

SEAFOOD CAN ALSO be served as a fondue, for a change; either with hot, creamy or spicy sauces or with cold mayonnaise and its variations.

Shellfish are delicious for a special occasion. But bite-sized fish cakes are good too, and make a quite inexpensive meal.

Chowders are thick fish soups very like stews. The word 'chowder' comes from the French 'chaudière', a large heavy pot which fishermen use for cooking. Chowders are included here because they can be kept hot like a fondue, and served into small individual bowls from a big central pot in much the same way.

PRAWNS, SHRIMPS AND SCAMPI

All these shellfish must be cooked and shelled before being used for a fondue or chowder. Fresh ones are usually sold already cooked. They are better to use, being firmer, than frozen or canned ones.

To boil freshly-caught prawns, shrimps or scampi

Cooked prawns should be colourful and have no spawn when cooked; much depends on their freshness and the way in which they are cooked. Wash well, then put into boiling salted water and keep them boiling for about 7–8 min. Dublin Bay prawns will take rather longer, shrimps only 5 min. They are ready when they begin to change colour. Do not overboil or they will become tasteless and indigestible.

To shell prawns or scampi

To shell prawns, take the head between the right-hand thumb and second finger, take the tip of the tail between the left thumb and forefinger, raise the shell at the knee or angle, pinch the tail and the shell will come apart, leaving the prawn attached to the head.

To shell shrimps

Take the head between the right thumb and forefinger and with the left forefinger and thumbnail raise on each side the shell of the tail, pinch the tail, and the shell will at once separate.

Note: 'Scampi' is the Venetian name for very large prawns, like Dublin Bay prawns. If you buy frozen, raw ones, cook them as soon as they are thawed.

PRAWN OR SCAMPI FONDUE

12 oz cooked, peeled prawns *or* **scampi** **Seasoned flour**	**Hot oil for frying** **Sauces of your choice** **(See below)**

Coat the shellfish thoroughly with seasoned flour. Serve a portion to each diner, to spear and dip in the hot oil himself.

Suggested sauces are Hollandaise Sauce (in a bowl standing in a container of hot water); Tartare Sauce; Mayonnaise verte.

3–4 helpings

SHRIMP FONDUE

Shrimps are too small to serve as fondue 'dippers' unless combined. Make them into rissolettes as below, and serve some to each diner, to dip in the one of the sauces listed.

2 oz cooked, peeled shrimps per person **Short crust pastry**	**Egg yolk** **Breadcrumbs** **Hot oil**

Wipe the shrimps dry. Roll out the pastry, thinly. Cut it into 1½–2-in rounds. Put a few shrimps in the centre of each round, and fold over into a crescent shape. Brush with beaten egg yolk, coat with breadcrumbs. Fry at the table until crisp and brown, drain well, and give a few to each guest, to dip into one of the following sauces:
Mushroom-Sour Cream Sauce; Mayon-naise; Tartare Sauce; Savoury Lemon Sauce.

MIXED FISH FONDUE

Serve each diner with bite-sized chunks of firm white or smoked fish, well dredged with seasoned flour, to fry for himself.

As sauces, serve Mayonnaise, Mushroom-Sour Cream Sauce, Tartare Sauce, Savoury Sauce.

FISH CAKES

1 lb cooked fish **1 oz butter** *or* **margarine** **½ lb mashed potatoes**	**2 eggs** **Salt and pepper** **Breadcrumbs**

Remove skin and bones and chop fish coarsely. Heat the butter in a saucepan, add the fish, potatoes, yolk of 1 egg, salt and pepper. Stir over heat for a few minutes, then turn on to a plate and allow to cool. When cold, shape into small, round flat cakes, brush over with beaten egg, coat with breadcrumbs and fry in hot fat.

3–7 helpings

QUICK FISH CAKES

One 1-pt pkt instant mashed potato, suitable for frying **½ lb cooked cod** *or* **haddock**	**1 tablesp tomato sauce**

Make up the potato as directed on the packet. Remove any skin and bones from the fish, flake and mix with the potato. Stir in the tomato sauce. Press or roll out the mixture to just over ¼ in thick and cut out with a plain cutter, about 2½ ins in diameter. Fry in deep or shallow fat until golden brown. Garnish with lemon curls and parsley sauce.

10–12 fish cakes

Mixed Seafood chowder

COD AND BACON CHOWDER

½ lb cod fillet
½ pt water
Salt and pepper
6 oz peeled, diced potato
2 oz lean bacon, finely shredded
6 oz onion, peeled and chopped
1 oz butter
1¼ pt milk
Fingers of hot, dry toast

Skin the fish. Place in a saucepan, and add water, salt and pepper. Bring to the boil, and simmer gently until the fish is cooked. Drain the fish, cool slightly and flake. Reserve the cooking liquid.

Cook the potato in the same liquid until tender. Drain.

In a frying pan, fry the bacon a little, enough to make the fat run. Add the onions, and fry for 2–3 min. Drain.

Heat the milk and a little of the fish cooking liquid in a clean pan. Add the fish, potato, bacon, onion and butter. Season well.

Bring to simmering (not boiling) point. Serve with fingers of hot, dry toast.

4 helpings

CRAB AND SWEET CORN CHOWDER

1 × 8 oz can creamed corn
4 oz cooked crab meat
1 small onion
2 rashers green (unsmoked) bacon
½ lb potatoes, peeled
1¼ pt milk
2 tablesp butter or margarine
2 tablesp double cream

Combine the corn and crab meat in a basin. Leave aside.

Cop the onion, and cut the bacon into small pieces. Dice the potatoes. Melt the butter in a saucepan, add the onion and bacon and fry gently for 2–3 min. Add the potatoes, and stir to coat with the fat. Add ½ pt water, bring to the boil and simmer until the potatoes are soft.

Add the corn and crab. Heat the milk, pour it into the main mixture and season well. Bring almost to the boil, stirring continuously.

Just before serving, add the cream.

MIXED SEAFOOD CHOWDER

1–1¾ lb smoked haddock *or* cod
1–2 finely chopped onions
1 breakfast cup instant mashed potato prepared with dried skim milk made up as liquid
2–3 skinned tomatoes
1–1½ oz butter *or* margarine
1 tablesp flour
3–4 tablesp dried skim milk made up as liquid
Salt and pepper
½ 10-oz can or pkt sweet corn kernels
¼ pt shelled prawns
1 dessertsp finely chopped parsley

Cover the haddock or cod with ¾ pt water, and bring gently to the boil. Remove the fish, skim any scum off the stock. Simmer the onions in a little of this stock until tender, and reserve the rest. Make up the potato if required. Cut the tomatoes into eighths and discard the seeds. Simmer them in the remaining stock until tender, then add them to the onions with the potato. Reserve the tomato stock. Free the fish of skin and bones. Melt the fat, add the flour and cook gently for 2–3 min without browning. Remove from the heat and slowly stir in the tomato stock. Cook for a few moments. Add the vegetables, fish stock and sweet corn. Then add the fish and most of the shellfish. Reserve a few prawns for garnish if liked. Heat the whole dish through without boiling. Turn into a serving dish, sprinkle with parsley, and garnish with the remaining shellfish if desired.

4–5 helpings

BOUILLABAISSE

This is the most famous of all fish soups, made chiefly in the South of France, different districts having particular recipes. It is a kind of thick stew of fish which should include a very wide mixture of different kinds of fish. In order to get a wide enough variety, a large quantity must be made.

A mixture of 8 to 10 different kinds of fish, e.g.:

Whiting	**John Dory**
Red mullet	**Monk fish**
Crawfish or	**Crab**
lobster	**Bass**
Conger eel or eel	**Sole**
Gurnet	

To every 2 lb fish allow:

1 large onion	**A sprig of savory**
1 leek	**A sprig of fennel**
1 clove of garlic	*or* **tarragon**
2 tomatoes	**1–8 teasp saffron**
1 bay leaf	**Salt and pepper**
A sprig of	**¼ pt olive oil**
parsley	**¼ pt white wine**

To each portion of bouillabaisse allow:

**1 thick slice of
french bread**

Clean the fish, cut them into thick slices and sort them into 2 groups, the firm-fleshed kind and the soft kind. Chop the onion; slice the leek; crush the garlic; scald; skin and slice the tomatoes. In a deep pan, make a bed of sliced vegetables and the herbs; season this layer. Arrange on top the pieces of firm-fleshed fish; season them and pour over them the oil. Add to the pan the wine and enough cold water or fish stock barely to cover the top layer of fish. Heat as quickly as possible to boiling point and boil briskly for 8 min. Now add the soft pieces of fish, forming a fresh layer. Boil for a further 5 min. Meanwhile, toast the slices of bread and arrange them in the bottom of the soup tureen or individual bowls. Pour the liquid over the bread and serve it as a fish bouillon. Serve the mixture of fish separately. The vegetables and herbs are for flavour only, and need not be served.

Dessert Fondues

DESSERT FONDUES are really sweet sauces in which the diners dip pieces of fruit, biscuits or small cookies. They are fun as a follow-up to a substantial casserole supper dish, or for a young people's party, but should never follow a main-dish fondue.

APRICOT FONDUE

1 lb dried apricots	3 tablesp Grand Marnier
Water	Parkin biscuits
8 oz castor sugar	
Good pinch of salt	

Wash the apricots, soak till soft, and then simmer till tender. Make a purée by sieving them. Place them in a fondue pan or saucepan, stir in the sugar, salt and a little water if very thick. Heat through. When very hot, stir in the liqueur. Serve with the biscuits for dipping.

BRANDY AND PEACH FONDUE

2 large eggs	½ gill peach brandy
4 oz sifted icing sugar	Fresh peaches, sliced
Pinch of salt	
1½ gills double cream	

Separate the eggs. Beat the whites until they stand in soft peaks. Gradually fold in the sugar, and beat again until very stiff. Beat the egg yolks and salt until fluffy. Fold into the egg white mixture. Beat the cream until stiff, and fold into the egg mixture with the brandy. Chill, and serve cold. Use the peach slices for dipping.

COFFEE AND BRANDY FONDUE

6 oz castor sugar	2 tablesp brandy
Generous ½ pt very strong black coffee	2 dessertsp butter
2 dessertsp cornflour	Shrewsbury biscuits

Melt the sugar slowly in the top of a double boiler, over hot water, stirring well. Slowly stir in all but 3 tablesp of the coffee. Blend the cornflour with the 3 tablesp cold coffee. Add to the mixture and stir until

Rich Chocolate Fondue ▶

the mixture comes to the boil and thickens. Remove from the heat, stir in the brandy and the butter. Serve warm, with the biscuits for dipping.

ORANGE FONDUE, HOT

5 oz castor sugar	1 teasp lemon
2 dessertsp	rind, grated
cornflour	¼ teasp vanilla
Pinch of salt	essence
¾ pt orange juice	2 tablesp
2 oz butter	Cointreau
2 tablesp grated	Mocha biscuits
orange rind	

Mix the sugar, cornflour and salt in the top of a double boiler. Stir in the orange juice gradually. Place the pan over simmering water. Bring slowly to the boil, while stirring. Cook until thick. Remove from the heat, and stir in the rest of the ingredients. Serve warm, with the biscuits for dipping.

RICH CHOCOLATE FONDUE

8 oz plain	2 tablesp kirsch
chocolate	Whole
4 oz milk	strawberries,
chocolate	apple slices
¼ pt evaporated	dipped in lemon
milk	juice or fresh
2 oz castor sugar	cherries
or as required	

Break the chocolate into pieces and combine in a saucepan with the milk and sugar, if you need it. Cook over very low heat until the chocolate is melted and smooth. Stir in the kirsch. Keep warm, and serve with the fruit for dipping.

SWISS CHOCOLATE FONDUE

12 oz Swiss milk	Whole
chocolate	strawberries or
½ pt double	cherries, or
cream	apple slices
2 tablesp kirsch	dipped in
	lemon juice for
	dipping

Break the chocolate into small pieces, and put in the top of a double boiler, over simmering water. When just melting, add the cream and kirsch. Stir until smooth. Serve with the strawberries, cherries or apple slices for dipping.

MORE SWEET FONDUE SAUCES

REMEMBER THAT you can also use most of these sauces as companions for sweet casseroles and 'bakes'.

BRANDY or RUM SAUCE

¼ pt single cream	⅛ pint brandy or
2 egg yolks	2 tablesp rum
1 dessertsp	
brown sugar	

Mix all the ingredients in a basin. Set the basin over a saucepan of hot water, and whisk until the mixture thickens.

BUTTERSCOTCH SAUCE

4 oz moist, dark	1 teasp
brown sugar	arrowroot
¼ pt water	A few drops of
1 oz butter	vanilla essence
1 strip of lemon	A few drops of
rind	lemon juice

Dissolve the sugar in the ¼ pt water, add the butter and lemon rind and boil for 5 min. Remove lemon rind. Blend the arrowroot with 2 teasp water; thicken the sauce with the blended arrowroot. Add vanilla and lemon juice to taste.

CARAMEL SAUCE

2 oz sugar or	½ pt custard
golden	sauce
syrup	Lemon juice or
⅛ pt water	vanilla essence

Put the sugar and 2 tablesp water in a small pan; dissolve the sugar over gentle heat, then boil the syrup so made until it is a deep golden-brown. Add to the caramel the rest of the water and leave it in a warm place to dissolve. If golden syrup is used heat it without water until of a golden-brown colour, then dissolve it in the water. Add the dissolved caramel to the custard sauce and flavour to taste.

CHOCOLATE SAUCE

¼ lb chocolate	1 teasp rum
½ pt milk	Sugar, if required
2–3 egg yolks	1 egg white
Vanilla essence	(optional)

Dissolve the chocolate in the milk. Make a custard with the egg yolks and the chocolate-flavoured milk. Flavour and sweeten to taste. If you like, one egg white may be whipped to a stiff froth and folded into the finished sauce.

CHOCOLATE SAUCE (COCOA)

2 rounded dessertsp cocoa	½ oz butter
	3 rounded dessertsp sugar
1 rounded dessertsp cornflour	½ pt water
	3 drops vanilla essence

Blend together the cornflour, cocoa and sugar with a little of the water. Boil remaining water and pour on to blended mixture. Return to pan and boil for 2 min, stirring all the time. Add vanilla and butter. Serve hot or cold.

CUSTARD SAUCE

1 dessertsp sugar	½ pt milk
2 egg yolks or 1 whole egg	Flavouring (See below)

Beat the egg yolks or whole egg slightly and beat in the sugar gradually. Warm the milk to about blood heat. Stir the milk into the egg mixture, return to the pan or place in the top of a double boiler, and heat very gently until the egg thickens. The mixture must not boil, or the egg will curdle. As soon as it thickens, pour the mixture through a strainer into a sauceboat or jug. Flavour and add extra sweetening if required.

If the custard *should* curdle, whisk it briskly with a fork just before serving.

Flavourings are legion. You can use almost any liqueur or essence, a powdered herb or spice such as cinnamon, or a bark or seeds such as a vanilla pod infused in the milk while it heats. Wine or fruit juice are other alternatives.

FRUIT SAUCE

Fruits suitable are: Damsons, Plums, Raspberries, Redcurrants, Blackberries.

1 lb bottled or fresh fruit	Lemon juice, if liked
A very little water to stew	1 teasp (rounded) arrowroot to each ½ pt purée
Sugar to sweeten	

Stew the fruit in the water till soft, then sieve it. Sweeten, flavour and thicken the sauce with arrowroot blended with a little cold water or fruit juice.

FRUIT SYRUP SAUCE (RASPBERRY)

6 lb sound ripe raspberries	½–¾ lb loaf sugar to each pt of juice

Crush the fruit in a jar standing in a pan of boiling water. Cook gently for about 1 hr to extract all the juice. Strain through a fine nylon sieve. Measure the juice and add the sugar. Bring back to the boil and cook for 15 min, removing the scum as it rises. Let stand until quite cold, then pour into bottles. Lock, seal, store and use as required.

Gooseberries, cranberries or strawberries can be used in the same way.

FRUIT AND YOGURT SAUCE—COLD

½ pt fruit purée	Sugar to sweeten
1 bottle plain yogurt	

Carefully mix the cold fruit purée and yogurt together. Sweeten well as the mixture will be very sour.

GINGER SYRUP SAUCE *(Method, p. 30)*

4 oz brown sugar	1 teasp arrowroot
½ pt water or ¼ pt syrup from preserved ginger and ¼ pt water	½ teasp ground ginger
	1 teasp lemon juice
Piece of root ginger	1 tablesp chopped preserved ginger
Strip of lemon rind	

opposite page top Red fruit sauce on pears
opposite page bottom Apple Loaf
top Lardy Cake
left Doughnuts

Dissolve the sugar in the water, add the root ginger and lemon rind and simmer for 15 min. Blend the arrowroot and ground ginger with a little cold water and the lemon juice, and with this thicken the sauce. Add the preserved ginger and simmer the sauce for 2–3 min.

LEMON SAUCE (CLEAR)

Rind of ½ lemon	Juice of 2 lemons
½ pt water	1 heaped teasp
4 oz sugar *or*	arrowroot
golden syrup to	
sweeten	

Infuse the thinly cut lemon rind in the water for 15 min, then remove it. Add sugar or syrup to flavour water and boil for 5 min. Add the lemon juice and thicken the sauce with the arrowroot blended with a little cold water.

Note: If you wish richer, a small glass of sherry and an egg yolk may be added to the above a few minutes before serving, but the sauce must not be allowed to boil again once the egg yolk has been added.

Make Orange Sauce in the same way, but with less sugar.

SABAYON SAUCE—HOT or COLD

2 egg yolks	¼ pt Marsala wine
1 oz castor sugar	*or* **Madeira**

In a saucepan whisk the egg yolks and sugar till very light and frothy. Stir in the wine and over very gentle heat continue whisking briskly until the sauce rises; it must not boil. Serve at once.

DIPPERS FOR DESSERT FONDUES

Most 'dippers' are baked goods, but pieces of fruit can also be used if not too moist.

APPLE LOAF

1 lb plain flour, sifted	1 cooking apple, peeled, cored and sliced
Pinch of salt	Milk to mix
1 teasp baking powder	

4 oz butter	4 oz icing sugar, sifted
4 oz lard	
2 eggs, beaten	A little water
2 oz currants	1 tart eating apple (red), cored and sliced
2 oz raisins, seeded	

Dip the fruit in a little lemon juice as soon as prepared, to prevent discoloration.

Sift together the flour, salt and baking powder. Rub in the fat, mix in the beaten egg, currants, raisins, cooking apple and milk. Mix well. Turn into a 1-lb lined loaf tin, and bake in a moderate oven at 190°C, 375°F, Gas 5, for 40–45 min, or until springy and browned. When cool, spread the loaf with a thin icing made with icing sugar and water, and decorate with sliced eating apple. Serve for high tea, especially when salads are scarce.

6–8 helpings

DOUGHNUTS

½ lb plain flour	1 egg
¼ teasp salt	Cinnamon sugar for coating
¾ oz lard and 1 oz margarine	
1 oz castor sugar	Fat for deep frying
½ oz yeast	
½–¾ gill warm milk	

Rub the fat into the warmed flour and salt; add sugar, having taken out ½ teasp to cream the yeast. Add the warm milk and egg to the creamed yeast and pour into the flour. Mix well (do not make too soft as the dough is to be cut out), and put to rise to double its size. Knead lightly and roll out ½ in thick. Cut into rings, using 2½–2¾-in cutter for outside and 1½–1¾-in for inner ring, and prove on a warm tray for 5 min. Drop into very faintly smoking fat and cook 5 min; drain well and toss in castor sugar *or* sugar mixed with ground cinnamon to taste.

Alternative method Divide dough into 12. Roll each piece into a ball and place a glacé cherry or a little jam in the middle. Prove 10 min and proceed as above.

14–16 doughnuts

BASIC SMALL 'RICH' CAKES

The following is a suitable mixture for all small cakes and can be varied in many ways.

2 oz butter *or* margarine	Pinch of salt
2 oz castor sugar	Water *or* milk as required
1 egg	
3 oz self-raising flour *or* 3 oz plain flour and 1 level teasp baking powder	

Beat the fat and sugar until creamy and white. Whisk the egg and add gradually; beat well between each addition. Sift together the flour, salt and baking powder. Gently stir the flour, etc., into the creamed fat; add milk or water to make a soft dropping consistency. Half-fill greased bun tins with the mixture and bake in a fairly hot to moderate oven (190–180 °C, 375–350 °F, Gas 5–4).

FLUTED ROLLS

Puff pastry trimmings	**Castor sugar**

Roll out the trimmings of pastry, dredge well with castor sugar and fold in three. Repeat this twice and then roll out to ¼-in thickness. Cut into rounds with a 2-in fluted cutter. Roll up, brush with water and sprinkle with castor sugar. Bake in a fairly hot oven (200 °C, 400 °F, Gas 6) till crisp and lightly browned.

This recipe is a practical one for using up pieces of frozen puff pastry, after making a slightly smaller tart than the packet supplies.

Cooking time 10 min

FRUIT 'DIPPERS'

The following are suitable; cut where required into 1-in cubes.

Pineapple chunks; melon 'fingers'; orange or tangerine segments, with pith removed; hulled strawberries; pear chunks marinated in lemon juice.

LARDY CAKE

1 lb white bread dough which has risen once	4 oz currants *or* sultanas
6 oz lard	A little spice, if liked
6 oz granulated sugar or a little less	Sugar syrup to glaze

Roll out the dough on a floured board, and put on half the lard in dabs, to cover two thirds of the surface, as in making flaky pastry. Sprinkle with the sugar, fruit and spices to your taste. Fold the dough into three, folding the unlarded piece over first. Turn to the right, and repeat the sugaring, larding and folding. Turn to the right again, and roll once more. Fold again. Roll, this time to fit a Yorkshire pudding tin about 12 × 7 in. Put to rise in a warm place, and cover with a clean tea towel. Due to the sugar, it will take longer than usual, but need only rise half its height. This will take about ¾ hr.

Bake in the centre of the oven at 200 °C, 400 °F, Gas 6, for about ¾ hr, until brown and crisp. When cooked (or before), brush with a thick sugar syrup to give a glistening top.

1 The cake looks better if you score the top with a sharp knife into diamond shapes before putting it to rise.

2 It is better eaten hot.

3 This is a traditional recipe, which used to be made on the day bread was baked, or from a piece of dough kept in the cold larder until the next day.

MACAROONS

2 egg whites	Rice paper *or* greaseproof
4 oz castor sugar	
3 oz ground almonds	Whole blanched almonds for top
1 teasp rice flour	
½ teasp vanilla essence	

Beat the egg whites stiffly in a large bowl. Mix the sugar, almonds and rice flour together and fold into the beaten whites; add the vanilla essence. Place the rice paper or greaseproof paper on a baking sheet. Put the mixture into a large bag with a $\frac{1}{2}$–1 in plain pipe and pipe on to the rice paper in rounds about 1$\frac{1}{2}$-in diameter. Place an almond in the centre of each round and bake in a moderate oven (180 °C, 350 °F, Gas 4).

20 macaroons　　　*Cooking time 20-30 mins*

MOCHA BISCUITS

5 oz butter	**1 tablesp liquid**
2 oz castor sugar	**coffee essence**
7 oz self-raising	**Beaten egg**
flour	
$\frac{1}{2}$ level teasp	
powdered	
cinnamon	

Cream the butter and castor sugar together until light and fluffy. Sift the flour and cinnamon and add to the butter and sugar together with the coffee essence. Work together. Using a forcing bag and rosette pipe, press out round and finger shapes on a greased baking sheet. Brush with beaten egg. Bake in a moderate oven (180 °C, 350 °F, Gas 4) for 25 min or until golden-brown.

PARKIN BISCUITS

2 oz plain flour	**1 oz lard** *or*
2 oz oatmeal	**hydrogenated**
1$\frac{1}{2}$ oz sugar	**shortening**
$\frac{1}{2}$ level teasp	**1 level teasp**
ground ginger	**bicarbonate of**
$\frac{1}{4}$ level teasp	**soda**
powdered	**1$\frac{1}{2}$ oz golden**
cinnamon	**syrup**
$\frac{1}{4}$ level teasp	**$\frac{1}{4}$ egg**
mixed spice	

DECORATION

Blanched almonds

Sift and mix flour, oatmeal, sugar and spices, and rub in the fat. Add soda, syrup and egg. Mix well to a fairly stiff consistency. Form into balls and place a little apart on greased baking sheets; put $\frac{1}{2}$ a blanched almond on top of each. Bake in a moderate to warm oven (180–170 °C, 350–335 °F, Gas 4–3). Allow to cool slightly before removing from sheet.

12-14 biscuits　　　*Cooking time 15-20 min*

Gingerbread

RICH DARK GINGERBREAD

8 oz plain flour	**2–4 oz crystallized**
$\frac{1}{8}$ teasp salt	**ginger**
1–2 level teasp	**2 oz blanched**
ground	**and chopped**
cinnamon	**almonds**
1–2 level teasp	**4 oz butter** *or*
mixed spice	**margarine**
2 level teasp	**4 oz sugar**
ground ginger	**4 oz treacle**
2 oz dates *or*	**2 eggs**
raisins, *or*	**A little warm**
sultanas	**milk, if**
1 level teasp	**required**
bicarbonate of	
soda	

Grease a 7-in tin and line the bottom with greaseproof paper, well greased, or silicone-treated paper.

Mix flour and salt and other dry ingredients with the prepared fruit, crystallized ginger cut into pieces, and almonds chopped roughly. Melt the fat, sugar and treacle, add to the dry ingredients with the beaten eggs. If the mixture seems stiff, add a little warm milk but do not make it too soft. Pour into the tin, and bake in a warm to cool oven (170–150 °C, 335–310 °F, Gas 3–2).

Cooking time 1$\frac{3}{4}$–2 hr

Mocha biscuits

What to Eat and Drink with Fondues

CHEESE FONDUES NEED only a crisp lightly-dressed green salad as accompaniment, although you can, of course, vary the breads you serve to suit the dish. All cheese fondues are rich, and filling enough by themselves otherwise.

Most people prefer salads with meat and seafood fondues too. But they can be more varied, including bite-sized snacks of blanched and raw vegetables (what the French call 'crudités'), and pickles and chutneys.

Do not try to serve a 'starter' course before a fondue. It is not needed, and in fact waiting for the cheese or hot oil to be ready is part of the fun. Don't spoil it.

As for drinks, most Swiss people drink tea with cheese fondues, with a quick digestive 'pick-up' of kirsch half-way through. But you could serve the same well-chilled white wine as you made the fondue with, or lager in summer. These drinks go well with seafood fondues and chowders too. But the heavier meat fondues need a red wine or some kind of cold or mulled ale.

Follow any fondue with fresh, well-polished fruit piled in a colourful pattern, or with the lightest of fruit desserts and sauces. Tea or coffee can end the meal.

Most of the salads in this section make just as good companions for hearty casseroles and 'bakes' as they do for fondues; in fact, most people prefer a salad to hot vegetables with these dishes.

SALADS, PICKLES AND CHUTNEYS

LETTUCE SALAD (PLAIN GREEN SALAD)

Lettuce, whether cabbage or cos, well prepared with a French dressing or Vinaigrette Sauce, provides the finest of all salads.

To prepare lettuce, cut off the stump of the lettuce and discard the coarse outer leaves only. Separate all leaves and wash them under running water. Put into a salad shaker or a clean tea-towel and swing them to shake out the water. Leave to drain.

The salads in which lettuce is used as a foundation are so numerous that it would be foolish to try to mention them all here.

APPLE AND CUCUMBER SALAD

1 cucumber	**Cream** *or*
3 dessert apples	**evaporated**
Salt and pepper	**milk**
Lemon juice	**Finely chopped**
	mint (optional)

Slice the cucumber thinly; quarter, core and slice the apples. Season lightly and sprinkle with lemon juice. Stir in a little cream or evaporated milk. Pile in a salad bowl. Sprinkle with a little mint, if liked.

Eat with seafood fondues.

6 helpings

BEETROOT SALAD

2 cooked	**Grated**
beetroots	**horseradish**
French dressing	

Slice or dice the beetroot and arrange neatly. Baste with French dressing, after sprinkling with freshly grated horseradish.

Dry mustard may be added to the dressing and the horseradish omitted for a red meat fondue.

For a more elaborate salad, add 2 peeled, cored and diced dessert apples, 2 oz shelled walnuts and 1 large celery heart, diced. Garnish with watercress.

6 helpings

BRUSSELS SPROUTS SALAD— COOKED

2 lb small,	
compact	
Brussels	
sprouts, cooked	
French dressing	
Beetroot	

Toss the sprouts lightly in the dressing and pile them in a salad bowl. Garnish with a border of diced or neatly sliced beetroot.

6 helpings

BRUSSELS SPROUTS SALAD— UNCOOKED

1 lb very young	**Salt**
Brussels sprouts	**French dressing**

Prepare the Brussels sprouts in the usual way, taking care to discard any coarse leaves. Shred very finely. Sprinkle with a little salt and dress with French dressing.

6 helpings

CARROT SALAD

3 large carrots	**Finely chopped**
1 lettuce	**parsley**
French dressing	

Grate the carrots finely and serve on a bed of lettuce leaves. Sprinkle with the French dressing. Garnish with chopped parsley.

Grated, raw carrot can be used with success

Beetroot salad

Chunky cucumber and yogurt salad

in many salads. It should be grated very finely to be digestible, and sprinkled with lemon juice or French dressing as soon as grated to retain its bright colour.

This goes well with a beef bourguignonne.

6 helpings

CHERRY SALAD

1 lb Morello cherries	**Finely chopped tarragon**
1 tablesp olive oil	**Finely-chopped chervil**
1 teasp lemon juice	**1 teasp castor sugar**
3 or 4 drops of tarragon vinegar	
1 dessertsp brandy *or* **Kirsch**	

Stone the cherries. Crack some of the stones and mix the kernels with the cherries. Mix the oil, lemon juice, vinegar, brandy or Kirsch, a very small quantity of tarragon and chervil and the sugar. Pour over the cherries.

4–6 helpings

CHUNKY CUCUMBER AND YOGURT SALAD

¼ pt plain yogurt	**2 cucumbers**
1 tablesp vinegar	**Paprika**
Sugar	

Mix the yogurt with the vinegar and a little sugar. Cut the cucumbers into 2 in lengths and stand upright on a dish. Pour the yogurt dressing over, sprinkle with paprika and serve with white meat fondues.

CAULIFLOWER SALAD

1 large cauliflower	**Vinaigrette sauce**

Steam the cauliflower then divide carefully into small sprigs. Arrange the sprigs neatly in a salad bowl and pour the sauce over while the cauliflower is still warm. Serve when quite cold with any meat fondue.

6 helpings

Cauliflower Salad and Mayonnaise, served here with jellied beef

'CRUDITÉS'

Simple vegetables, fruits (such as apples) and pickles make a colourful selection of bite-sized snacks. They may be uncooked, blanched, or cooked and served cold, and are usually presented in separate small dishes on a tray.

Raw and blanched vegetables should be cut up finely. Carrots should be grated, cabbage finely chopped and cauliflower broken into small sprigs. Other vegetables and fruits often served are:

sliced tomatoes	diced new
sliced cucumber	potatoes,
diced cooked	'dressed' while
beetroot	still warm, and
finely sliced raw	cooled
onion rings	celery curls
cooked green	gherkin fans
peas with	radish roses
tinned	tomato lilies
sweetcorn	shredded green
diced apple with	peppers
walnut fragments	
tossed in	
lemon juice	

ENDIVE SALAD

2 heads of endive
French dressing
  or **Vinaigrette**
  sauce

Prepare endive as *Lettuce*. Dress with French dressing and serve at once.

6 helpings

ENDIVE, CELERY AND BEETROOT SALAD

2 heads of endive	**Celery curls**
Salad dressing	**Cooked beetroot**
(bought)	**Fine cress**

Toss the tufts of endive in salad dressing and pile them in a salad bowl. Sprinkle with celery curls. Surround with a border of neatly sliced beetroot and tiny bunches of cress.

6 helpings

ENDIVE SALAD WITH BACON

2 heads of endive	2 tablesp vinegar
4 streaky rashers	(preferably
of bacon	wine vinegar)
Salt and pepper	

Use only the white hearts of the endive and divide the tufts into short pieces. Cut the bacon, with scissors, into fine shreds and fry it until golden brown. Drain on absorbent paper. Mix bacon with endive, add a little salt, freshly ground pepper, and the vinegar; mix thoroughly.

4–6 helpings

GRAPEFRUIT AND CHICORY SALAD

3 grapefruits	French dressing
3 small heads	made with
chicory	grapefruit juice
2 oz seedless	Fine cress
raisins	

Halve the grapefruits and remove the pulp in sections. Remove the partitions from the halved shells. Shred the chicory, reserving some neat rounds for garnish. Mix the grapefruit pulp, raisins and chicory lightly with the dressing. Fill the grapefruit shells with the mixture. Decorate with tiny bunches of cress and rounds of chicory. Serve with lamb, chicken or seafood.

6 helpings

GREEN SALAD
See **Lettuce Salad**

Note that you can use endive for a green salad in the same way as lettuce.

MELON SALAD

¼ of a medium-	1 bunch
sized melon	watercress
Salt and pepper	French dressing
Paprika pepper	Mayonnaise
1 teasp castor	Lemon
sugar	Cucumber
Lemon juice	

Cut the peeled melon into fine shreds. Mix lightly with seasoning, a pinch of paprika pepper, sugar, and a little lemon juice. Cover. If possible, leave on ice. Toss the watercress in French dressing. Pile the melon in a salad bowl, cover with mayonnaise. Decorate with thin slices of lemon and cucumber. Surround with a border of the watercress.

6 helpings

ORANGE SALAD

4 sweet oranges	Chopped
½ teasp castor	tarragon and
sugar	chervil *or*
1 tablesp French	chopped mint
dressing	

Peel the oranges thickly with a saw-edged knife, so that all pith is removed. Cut out the natural orange sections. Place in a salad bowl, sprinkle with sugar. Pour the dressing over and sprinkle with tarragon and chervil, or with chopped mint. Use with spicy meat fondues; good with ham.

4–6 helpings

TOMATO SALAD

6 large firm	Finely chopped
tomatoes	parsley
Salt and pepper	
French dressing	
or cream salad	
dressing	

Skin and slice the tomatoes. Season lightly. Pour the dressing over the tomatoes. Sprinkle with chopped parsley. Serve with meatballs.

6 helpings

TOMATO AND ONION SALAD

6 tomatoes	Salad dressing *or*
1 large onion	French dressing

Boil *or* bake the onion until almost tender. When cold chop it finely. Skin and slice the tomatoes, sprinkle the onion over them and add a little salad dressing or French dressing.

NOTE: 1 dessertsp finely-chopped chives, *or* 3 spring onions, finely chopped may be substituted for the cooked onion.

6 helpings

STUFFED TOMATO SALADS

| 6 large firm | Crisp lettuce |
| tomatoes | leaves |

STUFFING, choice of:

1 **Finely-shredded lettuce leaves; cold cooked asparagus tips; salad dressing** *or*
2 **Chopped celery; finely-diced cooked carrot; canned peas; salad dressing** *or*
3 **Chopped hard-boiled egg; chopped gherkins; salad dressing** *or*
4 **Chopped shrimps** *or* **prawns; finely-shredded lettuce leaves; salad dressing**

Cut off the tops of the tomatoes, take out the centres and the pulp. Use a little of the pulp with the stuffing. Mix the chosen stuffing and fill the tomatoes. Put back the tops. Garnish with tiny sprigs of parsley or with a suitable ingredient of the filling. Dish on crisp lettuce leaves on individual dishes or plates.

6 helpings

SPICED PICKLING VINEGAR

Buy only the best bottled vinegar for pickling, with an acetic acid content of at least 5 per cent. It is false economy to buy cheap vinegar: if—as is often the case—the percentage of acetic acid is too low the pickles will not keep.

For home use, the flavour of malt vinegar is usually preferred.

To make spiced vinegar, add to 1 qt of vinegar: $\frac{1}{2}$ oz cloves, $\frac{1}{2}$ oz allspice, $\frac{1}{2}$ oz ginger, $\frac{1}{2}$ oz cinnamon, $\frac{1}{2}$ oz white pepper.

NOTE: All these spices should be whole, not ground. Buy them fresh. If you find this spice too strong, reduce the quantities. Steep the spices in the unheated vinegar for 1–2 months. Shake the bottle occasionally. Then strain and re-cork the bottle until needed.

Quick method If the spiced vinegar is wanted immediately, put the spices and vinegar into a basin. Bring the basin with a plate and stand it in a saucepan of cold water. Bring the water to the boil, remove the pan from the heat, and allow the spices to remain in the warm vinegar for about 2 hr. Keep the plate on top of the basin so that no flavour is lost. Strain the vinegar and use, either cold or hot according to the recipe.

PICKLED BEETROOT

Beetroots are obtainable most of the year and, like all the root crops, require cooking before pickling. Wash off any soil still clinging to the roots, taking care not to break the skin, for beetroot bleeds easily. If pickling for immediate use, simmer for $1\frac{1}{2}$–2 hr. When cold, skin and cut into squares or slices, and cover with unspiced or spiced vinegar, whichever is preferred.

If pickling for storage, bake the roots in a moderate oven (180 °C, 350 °F, Gas 4) until tender and, when cold, skin and cut into squares—it packs better that way for keeping; cover with spiced vinegar to which has been added $\frac{1}{2}$ oz salt to each pint Beetroot contains a good deal of sugar, and fermentation is more likely than with other vegetables, so seal thoroughly to exclude air.

PICKLED CUCUMBER

The easiest way to pickle cucumbers is to quarter them lengthways, cut into smaller pieces, brine with dry salt for 24 hr, then pack and cover with spiced vinegar. Like most vegetables they are best mixed with others.

PICKLED GHERKINS

These need a longer process, especially if their deep green colour is to be fixed. They need partial cooking.

Choose gherkins of a uniform size, place in a saucepan and cover with standard brine ($\frac{1}{2}$ lb salt to 3 pt water). Bring to near boiling-point; do not actually boil, but simmer for 10 min.

Drain until cold, then pack into jars and cover with spiced vinegar, preferably aromatic.

A great many people prefer sweet gherkins; they are particularly popular at cocktail

Pickled onions and beetroot

Green Salad

parties. These are quite easy to prepare from the ordinary pickled fruit.

A spoonful of sugar added to the jar and shaken up, then allowed to stand for 24 hr, is all that is needed. Do not do this too-long in advance as sugar added to a cold pickle in this way may very easily start to ferment. Another way is to turn the gherkins out on to a shallow dish, the one in which they will be served, and sprinkle with sugar an hour or two before serving.

MIXED PICKLES

Make a selection of available vegetables. Any of the following are suitable: small cucumbers, cauliflower, small onions, French beans. Prepare the vegetables: only the onions need be peeled, the rest should merely be cut into suitably sized pieces.

Put all into a large bowl, sprinkle with salt, and leave for 24 hr. Drain thoroughly and pack into jars. Cover with cold spiced vinegar, seal, and leave for at least a month before using.

PICKLED NASTURTIUM SEEDS

Nasturtium seeds when pickled are a good substitute for capers, and add variety to salad dressings. They are rather too small to be popular on the table, but go well in mixed pickles.

Gather seeds whilst still green on a dry day and steep in brine ($\frac{1}{2}$ lb salt to 3 pt water) for 24 hr. Pack in small jars, warm in the oven for 10 min and cover with hot spiced vinegar. It is best to use a hot spice mixture for these, and a few leaves of tarragon, if available.

Mixed pickles

The only important thing to remember is to use small jars or bottles, so that they are consumed at once when opened.

PICKLED ONIONS

Use small even-sized pickling onions. Peel with a stainless knife and drop them into a basin of salted water until all have been peeled. Remove from water and allow to drain thoroughly before packing into jars or bottles. Cover with cold spiced vinegar and keep for at least 1 month before using.

PICKLED WALNUTS

Use walnuts whose shells have not begun to form. Prick well with a silver fork; if the shell can be felt, do not use the walnut.

The shell begins to form opposite the stalk, about $\frac{1}{4}$ in from the end.

Cover with a brine (1 lb salt to 1 gal water) and leave to soak for about 6 days. Drain, make fresh brine, and leave to soak for a further 7 days.

Drain, and spread in a single layer on dishes, leaving exposed to the air, preferably in sunshine, until the nuts blacken (1–2 days). Pack into jars and cover with hot spiced vinegar. Tie down when cold and leave for at least a month before using.

Wear gloves when handling walnuts.

APPLE CHUTNEY (*Method, p. 42*)

6 lb apples	**3 pt vinegar**
2 lb sultanas	**$3\frac{1}{2}$ lb sugar**
$\frac{3}{4}$ lb preserved ginger	**1 oz salt**
	1 teasp allspice

Peel, core and chop the apples into small pieces and chop up the sultanas and ginger. Mix the vinegar, sugar, salt and spice together and bring to the boil, then add the apples and simmer for 10 min before adding the ginger and sultanas. Simmer until the mixture becomes fairly thick, then pour into the jars.

BENTON KETCHUP OR SAUCE

¼ pt vinegar, preferably wine	1 teasp mixed mustard
2 tablesp grated horseradish	1–2 teasp castor sugar

Mix all the ingredients well together. This sauce will keep for a month. Serve with beef.

BRISBANE APRICOT AND SULTANA CHUTNEY

1 lb dried apricots	1½ pt cider vinegar
1½ lb onions	1 dessertsp salt
1 lb granulated sugar	2 gloves garlic, crushed
Grated rind and juice of 2 oranges	1 teasp mustard
½ lb sultanas	½ teasp powdered allspice

Soak the apricots overnight, then drain and chop them. Finely chop or mince the onions. Put the apricots and onions in a preserving pan with the sugar, rind and juice of the oranges, the sultanas and the cider vinegar. Add the salt, garlic, mustard and allspice. Simmer until soft, stirring occasionally to prevent sticking. Pour into hot jars, cover and seal.

5–6 lb chutney

TOMATO KETCHUP

6 lb ripe tomatoes	½ teasp cloves
1 pt vinegar	½ teasp cinnamon
½ lb sugar	½ teasp cayenne pepper
1 oz salt	
½ teasp allspice	

Cut the tomatoes into quarters, place them in a preserving pan with the salt and vinegar and simmer until the tomatoes are quite soft and broken up. Strain the mixture through coarse muslin or a nylon sieve, then return the purée to the preserving pan and add the sugar. Continue to simmer till the ketchup starts to thicken, and then add the spices a little at a time, stirring thoroughly until the flavour is to taste.

When the ketchup is reasonably thick, fill into hot bottles and seal immediately, or allow it to cool slightly, then fill the bottles and sterilise at 80 °C, 170 °F, for 30 min.

Remember it will be thicker when cold than hot, so don't reduce it too far.

GREEN TOMATO CHUTNEY

5 lb green tomatoes	1 lb sugar
1 lb onions	1 qt vinegar
½ oz peppercorns	½ lb raisins
1 oz salt	½ lb sultanas

Slice the tomatoes and chop the onions and mix together in a basin with the peppercorns and salt. Allow this to stand overnight. Next day boil up the sugar in the vinegar, then add the raisins (which may be chopped) and the sultanas. Simmer for 5 min, then add the tomatoes and onions, and simmer till thick.

QUEENSLAND FRUIT CHUTNEY

4 lb apples	1 level teasp cayenne pepper
2 lb pears	
3 lb tomatoes	1 teasp cloves
1 level teasp mace	1 teasp peppercorns
½ lb sultanas	
½ lb seedless raisins	2 tablesp salt
4 lb sugar	1 teasp ground ginger
2 qt vinegar	

Peel the apples and pears, core them and cut them into small pieces. Skin the tomatoes and add them to the apples and pears. Add the remainder of the ingredients, and simmer for two hours. Bottle while hot, and seal when cold.

About 10 lb chutney

BAGELS

½ oz yeast	1 teasp salt
1 oz castor sugar	1 egg
2 oz margarine	1 lb flour
1½ teacups water	Poppy seeds

Cream the yeast with 1 teasp of the sugar. Put the margarine, water, salt and remaining sugar in a saucepan and place over a gentle heat until margarine is melted; leave till just lukewarm, then mix in the dissolved yeast. Add this mixture with the beaten egg to the flour and knead to a firm dough. Cover with a cloth and leave in a warm place till just beginning to rise. Knead again and roll into small pieces the width of a finger and about 5 in long. Shape into rings, pinching the ends well together, and leave again on a floured board in a warm place until beginning to rise. Then drop a few at a time in a saucepan ½ full of boiling water and cook gently till they rise to the top. Remove with a fish-slice on to greased baking sheets and sprinkle with poppy seeds. Bake in a fairly hot oven (190 °C, 375 °F, Gas 5) till golden-brown and crisp —20–30 min.

20 bagels

BAKING-POWDER BREAD

1 lb plain flour	Milk to mix to
1 teasp salt	light spongy
2 oz lard *or*	dough—average
margarine	½ pt
2 round *or* 4 level	
teasp baking	
powder	

Sift the flour and salt and rub in the fat until quite fine. Add the baking powder and mix very lightly with the milk. Shape into small loaves or bake in two greased 6-in cake tins. Put into a hot oven (230–220 °C, 450–425 °F, Gas 8–7).

Cooking time—(Small loaves)—10–15 min
(Large loaves)—25–30 min

BASIC MILK BREAD

1 lb plain flour	½ pt warm milk
1 teasp salt	(approx)
½ oz yeast	1 egg (optional)
½ teasp sugar	
2 oz lard *or*	
margarine	

Mix the salt with the warmed flour, cream the yeast with the sugar. Rub fat into flour and mix with the yeast, milk and egg if used, to a fairly soft, light dough. Beat until mixture is smooth and leaves the sides of the basin clean. Allow to stand in a warm place till twice its original size. Proceed as for White Bread.

Bread plait Roll risen dough into two strips, each 10 in long by 5 in or 6 in wide. Cut each strip almost to the top in three even-sized pieces and plait them as if plaiting hair. Damp and seal the ends neatly but firmly and place on a greased baking sheet. Allow to prove 10–15 min. Brush with egg wash and place in a hot oven (230 °C, 450 °F, Gas 8). Bake 20–30 min, reducing heat after first 10 min to 200 °C, 400 °F, Gas 6 or 190 °C, 375 °F, Gas 5.

2 loaves   *Cooking time 20–30 min*

BASIC WHITE BREAD

3½ lb white flour	1 teasp sugar
3½ teasp salt	1¾ pt warm
1 oz yeast	water

Grease 3–4 loaf tins and put them to warm. Mix salt and flour well together, cream yeast with the sugar and add to warm water. Make a well in the centre of the flour, pour the liquid into the well and sprinkle on or mix in a little of the flour to form a pool of batter and allow to stand in a warm place for 20 min. Mix to an elastic dough, using more water if required; knead well till the dough leaves the basin clean, and put to rise in a warm place until the dough has doubled its size. Then turn on to a floured board, knead again not too heavily but until there are only small holes in the dough, and put into the prepared tins. Put to prove until the

Ingredients for chutneys

dough is well up the sides of the tin the bake in a hot oven (220 °C, 425 °F, Gas 7).

3–4 loaves　　　　　　*Cooking time 1 hr*

Nut bread Make like white bread. Add 8 oz chopped nuts (walnuts, peanuts, etc.).

Raisin bread Make like white bread. Add 8 oz chopped raisins when kneading the dough for the second time.

Sultana bread Make like white bread. Add 8 oz sultanas when kneading the dough for the second time.

BOSTON BROWN BREAD
(Steamed)

3½ oz wholewheat flour	4 teasp baking powder
3 oz rolled oats, minced *or* passed through electric blender	¼ pt black treacle
	½ pt warmed sour milk *or* buttermilk
1 teasp salt	
3 oz fine semolina	

Mix all the dry ingredients in a basin. Mix the treacle with the milk, and beat it into the dry ingredients gradually. Grease two ½-lb cocoa tins thoroughly inside. Pour in the batter, filling each tin not more than half-full. Seal the tops. Place in a saucepan containing enough boiling water to come half-way up the sides of the tins. Simmer for 3½ hr. Allow to stand in the tins for at least 10 min before turning out the bread. To turn out, cut the bottoms off the tins.

2 small loaves

CROISSANTS

1 lb plain flour	1 egg, beaten
2 level teasp salt	4–6 oz hard
1 oz lard	margarine

YEAST MIXTURE

1 oz fresh yeast blended into ½ pt (less 1 tablesp) water *or* 1 level tablesp dried yeast sprinkled on the same amount of water warmed to 43 °C, 110 °F, with 1 teasp sugar

Rub the 1 oz lard into the flour. Make a dough with the yeast mixture after letting it stand for 10 min. Mix the beaten egg in with the yeast mixture. Knead the dough on a lightly floured board for 10–15 min until smooth. Roll into a strip about 20 × 8 in and ¼ in thick, taking care to keep the edges straight and corners square. Soften the margarine with a knife, and divide it into 3 parts. Dot one part in flakes over two-thirds of the dough, leaving a small border clear. Fold in 3, folding over the unflaked portion first. Turn the dough so that the fold is on the right-hand side. Seal the edges with a rolling pin. Re-shape into a long strip by gently pressing the dough at intervals with a rolling pin. Repeat the flaking and folding process twice more. Place the finally shaped dough in a polythene bag, and let it rest in the refrigerator for ½ hr. Roll out as before, and repeat the folding process 3 times more. Let the dough rest in the fridge for 1 hr this time.

Roll the dough into a rectangle about 23 × 14 in. Let it rest for 10 min. Then trim it with a knife to 21 × 12 in and divide the strip in half lengthways. Cut each strip into 6 triangles 6 in high with a 6 in base. Make an egg wash with 1 egg, a little water and ½ teasp sugar. Brush the croissants. Roll up each triangle loosely towards its point from the opposite side, ending with the tip underneath. Curve each into a crescent moon shape.

Put the shaped croissants on an ungreased baking sheet. Brush the tops with egg wash, put the sheet into a lightly greased polythene bag and leave at room temperature for about ½ hr, until the croissants are light and puffy. Brush yet again with egg wash, and bake in the centre of a hot oven at 220°C, 425°F, Gas 7, for 20 min.

FANCY BREAD ROLLS

½ lb plain flour	1 heaped teasp
1 level teasp salt	castor sugar
1 oz margarine	¼ pt skim milk
½ oz fresh yeast	made from
or ¼ oz dried	milk powder
yeast	

Sift the flour and salt into a large bowl. Leave to stand in a warm place for 10–15 min. Rub in the margarine. Cream the yeast and sugar together until liquid. Warm the milk and stir it into the yeast mixture. Make a well in the centre of the flour, pour in the liquid and mix to a soft dough. Knead for 5–10 min on a floured surface, until the dough is smooth and glossy. Place in a greased bowl, turn over to grease the whole surface of the dough, cover with a damp cloth, and leave to rise until doubled in size. Shape as required.

Trefoils Divide the basic dough into 8 pieces, then divide each piece into 3 bits. Form these into balls and cluster 3 together in a patty tin. Fill 8 tins, then leave in a warm place until doubled in size. It will take about 15 min. Brush with beaten egg yolk and skim milk to glaze, and scatter on a few poppy seeds. Bake in a fairly hot oven, at 200°C, 400°F, Gas 6, for 15–20 min.

Bread knots Divide the dough into 8 pieces and roll each into a tube shape about 10 in long. Tie in a loose knot. Prove and

Bottling Queensland fruit chutney

glaze as above, place on a greased baking sheet, and bake like trefoils.

Baby cottage loaves Divide the basic dough into 8 pieces. Cut each piece into a smaller and larger piece. Shape into rounds. Place the larger rounds on a greased baking sheet, and put the smaller ones on top. Make a dip in the centre of each with your finger. Prove and glaze like trefoils, and bake in the same way.

Ginger twists Knead 2 level teasp ground ginger into the dough (or sift in with the flour). Divide the dough into 16 pieces and roll each out 6 in long. Twist 2 pieces together, and place on a greased baking sheet. Prove, glaze and bake like trefoils. When cooked and cool, brush over with icing made from sifted icing sugar and water.

GRISSINI BREAD or SALT STICKS

1 lb plain flour	½ oz yeast
1 teasp salt	½ teasp sugar
Enough warm	3–4 tablesp
water to make	warm milk
a fairly stiff	
dough	

Make as for Milk Bread; allow to rise for 1–1½ hr. Form into long sticks 6–8 in. in length and when proved brush with egg white, bake in a hot oven (220 °C, 425 °F, Gas 7) until crisp.

If liked, they may be brushed with milk and sprinkled with a little coarse salt before baking.

12 sticks　　　　*Cooking time 20–30 min*

MALTED BROWN BREAD

3½ lb wholemeal	3 teasp salt
flour	1¾ pt warm
¾ oz yeast	water (approx)
1 oz malt extract	

Put the flour into a large bowl and make a well in the centre. Mix the yeast and malt extract in the warm water and pour into the well. Stir in about ¼ of the flour to make a pool of batter (setting the sponge), cover with a clean cloth and leave in a warm place (probably the warmth of the kitchen will do) for 30 min to 1 hr. At the end of the time sprinkle the salt well round the dry flour and mix all to an elastic dough, knead well, and form into loaves. Put into warmed greased tins and prove till risen well up the tins. Bake in a hot oven (230–220 °C, 450–425 °F, Gas 8–7).

3–4 loaves　　　*Cooking time 45–60 min*

MUFFINS

The traditional English muffins made in the North Country use a very plain yeast dough.

Yeast liquid

½ oz fresh yeast blended in ½ pt warm water *or* 2 level teasp dried yeast sprinkled in ½ pt warm water with 1 teasp sugar and allowed to stand until frothy, in about 10 min

Other ingredients

1 lb plain	1 teasp salt
flour	

Prepare the yeast liquid. Mix flour and salt. Add yeast liquid all at once and work to a fine dough, until sides of bowl are clean. Turn dough on to a lightly floured surface, and knead until dough is firm and elastic, in about 10 min. Place dough in a large polythene bag, lightly oiled inside, and allow to rise until double in size, and when dough springs back if pressed with a floured finger.

Rising takes about:
45 min in a warm place
2 hr at average room temp
up to 12 hr in a cold larder, *or*
up to 24 hr in a refrigerator

Turn the risen dough on to a lightly floured surface and knead lightly again. Roll out to ½ in thickness. Leave to rest for 5 min, covered with a sheet of polythene, then cut into 3½-in rounds. Re-roll and cut remains until all the dough is used. Cook on a hot greased griddle for about 6 min on each side until golden-brown, *or* bake in a hot oven, 230 °C, 450 °F, Gas 8, for 10 min, turning over with palette knife after 5 min.

NOTE: Muffins should be pulled open all round, with the fingers. Toast slowly on both sides. Then pull them wholly apart, butter well, put together again and serve hot.

OATMEAL BREAD

Oatmeal Bread, known as Clapbread in Lancashire, is an old English bread, which goes particularly well with cheese. It keeps fresh and moist for several days, and is good toasted.

Yeast liquid

1 oz fresh yeast in $\frac{1}{8}$ pt water

or

1 teasp sugar in $\frac{1}{8}$ pt water and 2 level teasp dried yeast

Blend the fresh yeast and water, or sprinkle the sugar in the water warmed to 110 °F, then sprinkle on the dried yeast. Leave until frothy, in about 10 min.

Other ingredients

$\frac{1}{2}$ **lb oatmeal**	**1 level tablesp**
(fine, medium	**salt**
or rolled)	**2 tablesp oil,**
$\frac{1}{2}$ **pt milk**	**melted butter**
12 oz plain flour	*or* **margarine**

Soak the oatmeal in the milk for $\frac{1}{2}$ hr. Prepare the yeast liquid above. Mix the soaked oatmeal, flour, salt and oil or butter or margarine together. Add the yeast liquid and work to a firm but soft dough, adding extra flour if needed until the dough leaves the bowl clean. Turn the dough on to a lightly floured surface, and knead thoroughly until it feels smooth and elastic. It will take about 10 min.

Put the dough to rise inside an oiled polythene bag, loosely tied at the top, until it doubles in size and springs back when pressed with a floured finger. Rising times can be varied to suit your convenience:

45–60 min in a warm place
2 hr at room temp
12 hr in a cold room or larder
24 hr in a refrigerator

Refrigerated dough must be allowed to return to room temperature before shaping.

Turn the risen dough on to a lightly floured surface, knead lightly and divide into two portions. Flatten each piece and roll up like a Swiss roll, shaped to fit a 1-lb loaf tin. Place the shaped dough in 2 1-lb bread tins, greased. Put the tins inside a large polythene bag until the dough rises to the tops of the tins.

Brush the tops of the loaves with milk and

sprinkle with oatmeal. Bake on the middle shelf of the oven at 230 °C, 450 °F, Gas 8, for 30 min. Turn down to 150 °C, 300 °F, Gas 1–2, and bake a further 30 min. Remove from the tins and cool on a wire tray.

Alternative shapes

1 Shape the two pieces of dough to form a large bun, flatten slightly, brush with milk and dredge with flour or oatmeal. Cook on a floured baking sheet, as above.

2 Flatten the bun shapes to 1 in thickness, cut into 6 pieces, brush with milk and dredge with flour or oatmeal. Bake on a baking sheet dredged with flour or oatmeal as above.

Both these shapes will take less time to bake than in the bread tins.

NUT AND RAISIN BREAD (Wholemeal)

$\frac{3}{4}$ **lb wholemeal**	**2 oz sugar**
flour	**2 oz sultanas**
$\frac{1}{4}$ **teasp salt**	**4 oz chopped**
2 oz lard	**nuts**
2 round teasp	**1 egg**
baking powder	$\frac{1}{2}$ **pt milk**

Rub the fat into the sifted flour and salt. Add remaining dry ingredients and mix to a fairly soft dough with egg and milk. Put into a well-greased bread or cake tin and bake in a faily hot oven (200–190 °C, 400–375 °F, Gas 6–5).

1 loaf　　　　　　　*Cooking time 1 hr*

PARKER HOUSE ROLLS

$\frac{3}{4}$ **lb plain flour**	$1\frac{1}{2}$ **gills milk**
1 teasp salt	**2 tablesp cold**
6 teasp baking	**water**
powder	**Softened butter**
3 tablesp *or*	
$1\frac{1}{2}$ **oz melted**	
butter *or*	
other fat	

Sift the dry ingredients into a basin. Mix the melted butter and milk and water, and pour the mixture slowly into the dry ingredients, stirring it to a soft dough. Toss or lift strands of dough two or three times with a fork, then place dough on a lightly floured board. Roll out $\frac{1}{2}$ in thick, and cut into rounds. Crease across the centre with the back of a knife. Brush with softened butter, and fold over along the crease. Place rolls on a greased baking sheet 1 in apart, and cover with a warm cloth. Stand in a warm place for 10 min. Brush the tops with softened butter. Bake at 230 °C, 450 °F, Gas 8, for about 15 min, or until puffy and browned.

REFRIGERATOR ROLLS

These rolls are so easy to make that even a beginner succeeds with them. The dough can be kept in the refrigerator for 4–5 days, and a portion can then be used each day, to make fresh rolls. This is an ideal plan for people living alone, or for small families, since it enables them to have fresh bread every day without any trouble.

Croissants

8 fl oz or 1½ gills plus 2 tablesp hot milk	**1 cake compressed yeast**
1 tablesp castor sugar	**3 tablesp warm water**
1 teasp salt	**1 egg, beaten**
2 tablesp lard	**14 oz plain flour**
	Softened butter

Mix the hot milk with the sugar, salt and fat. Cool until lukewarm. Cream the yeast, and mix with the warm water. Stir it into the milk mixture. Add the egg and mix thoroughly. Stir in the flour gradually. Mix with a wooden spoon until blended; do not knead. Place the dough in a greased bowl. Brush the top with softened butter to prevent a crust forming. Cover tightly, then store in the refrigerator for at least 24 hr before use.

To use: take out a portion of dough, and let it come to room temperature, in about $\frac{1}{2}$ hr. Shape into rolls. Place on the greased baking sheet or in deep bun tins. Space well apart and only fill tins half-full. Let dough rise until double its size. Bake at 220 °C, 425 °F, Gas 7, for 15–20 min.

RYE BREAD

Rye flour is obtainable from Health Food Stores and may be coarse when the whole grain is included, or fine when some of the outer layers of the grain are removed. The coarse rye flour gives a closer, heavier texture.

10 oz rye flour	**¼ pt warm milk**
10 oz plain white flour	**1 tablesp black treacle**
½ oz salt	**1 oz fresh yeast** or
1 level teasp sugar	**1 level tablesp dried yeast**
6 fl oz warm water	

Starch glaze

2 teasp cornflour blended with a little cold water. Stir in half a cup of boiling water to clear

Prepare yeast liquid by blending the fresh yeast in the warm water and add the milk, heated to lukewarm with the treacle or stir 1 level teasp of sugar into the warm water (about 43 °C or 110 °F) and sprinkle on the dried yeast. Leave until frothy, about 10 min. Add the milk, heated to lukewarm with the treacle. Mix dry ingredients together in a large mixing bowl. Add the yeast liquid to the dry ingredients and mix

Scotch pancakes

to form a firm dough adding extra flour if required. Turn the dough on to a lightly floured board and knead until the dough feels smooth and elastic about 10 min. Leave the dough to rise, in a lightly greased polythene bag, until it doubles in size:

1¼–1½ hr in a warm place
2 hr at room temp
12–24 hr in a refrigerator

Turn the risen dough on to a lightly floured board, divide into two and shape each piece into a cob or baton. Place on a greased baking tray, cover with a sheet of lightly greased polythene and leave to rise in a warm place until doubled in size, and the dough springs back when lightly pressed with a floured finger:

40–50 min in a warm place
1–2 hr at room temp
Overnight in the refrigerator

Remove polythene and brush top with starch glaze. Heat the oven to 230 °C, 450 °F, Gas 8. Place loaves on middle shelf of oven and turn oven to 200 °C, 500 °F, Gas 6. Bake for 30 min. Remove from oven and brush with starch glaze again. Turn oven down to 150 °C, 300 °F, Gas 2, and bake for a further 15 min. Re-glaze and bake for a final 5 min.

SCOTCH PANCAKES OR GIRDLE SCONES

4 oz self-raising flour
Pinch of salt
1 oz sugar
1 egg
¼ pt milk
1 oz margarine, melted

Sift together the flour, salt and sugar. Add the beaten egg, and then milk. Mix well. Stir in the melted margarine.

Drop the mixture in spoonfuls on a hot griddle, electric hot-plate or frying pan, and cook for 2 min on each side. Keep warm in a folded tea towel until needed.

SCOTTISH BROWN BREAD
(Wholemeal) *(Method, p. 50)*

3¼ lb wholemeal flour
¼ lb oatmeal
3½ teasp salt
1 teasp sugar
1 oz yeast
2 level teasp bicarbonate of soda
1½–1¾ pt warm water (approx)

Mix the wholemeal flour and oatmeal and proceed as for wholemeal bread below, adding soda dissolved in a little water. Prepare tins by greasing and dusting very thickly with flour. Oval-shaped tins give an attractive-looking loaf. Divide the dough into pieces and put in tins. Press well into shape and smooth on top. Prove for 15 min or until well risen, with a baking-sheet on top. Bake in a very hot oven (230°C, 450°F, Gas 8) with a baking sheet and weight on top, reducing the heat after 20 min to fairly hot (190°C, 375°F, Gas 5). The finished bread should be floury on the outside.

3-4 loaves   *Cooking time 45-60 min*

SOUR MILK BREAD

1 lb plain flour	½ pt sour milk
1 teasp salt	*or* buttermilk
1 round *or* 2	(approx)
level teasp	2 oz lard may be
bicarbonate of	rubbed in; this
soda	makes a better
1 round *or* 2 level	keeping bread
teasp cream of	
tartar	

Sift the flour and salt, and, if you wish, rub in the fat. Add the soda and tartar, making quite sure that all the lumps are sifted out of the soda. Mix to a light spongy dough with the milk. Divide the dough and form into two round cakes. Place on a greased baking sheet and bake in a hot oven (230–220°C, 450–425°F, Gas 8–7).

2 loaves   *Cooking time 30 min*

VIENNESE BREAD

Yeast liquid

1½ oz fresh yeast in ¾ pt warm water
or
1 teasp sugar in ¾ pt warm water and 1 level tablesp, plus 2 level teasp dried yeast

Blend fresh yeast and water, or sprinkle dried yeast on the sugar and water. Leave until frothy, about 10 min.

Dry mix

1½ lb strong flour	1 level teasp
2 level teasp salt	sugar
2 level tablesp	1 oz lard
dried milk	

Prepare the yeast liquid. Sift flour and salt together. Add the dried milk. Rub in the lard. Add the yeast liquid, and work to a firm dough until the sides of the bowl are clean. Turn the dough on to a lightly floured board, and knead until firm, elastic and no longer sticky. It will take about 10 min. Ideally dough temperature should be 80°F at this stage. Shape the dough into a ball and place in a large, oiled polythene bag, loosely tied at the top. Allow to rise until doubled in size, and till dough springs back when pressed with a floured finger. It is best to raise this dough at room temperature, away from too much warmth. It will take about 2 hr to rise at room temperature. Turn the risen dough on to a lightly floured board, and knead to knock out the air bubbles. Cover, and allow the dough to relax for 10 min before shaping.

To shape dough Divide the dough into 5 equal pieces, about 8 oz in weight. Mould each dough piece as tightly as possible, avoiding breaking the skin. If this happens, stop moulding and allow dough to recover again, and then mould lightly into a torpedo shape about 9 in long. Taper slightly at the ends.

Place loaves on lightly greased trays, and cover with a polythene sheet or bag. This helps to prevent skinning. Raise the dough away from draughts until it is fully risen and springs back when pressed with a floured finger. Cut three or four diagonal slits across the loaves with a razor blade, and place immediately in the oven, preheated to 230°C, 450°F, Gas 8. Place two baking tins of water in the bottom of the oven to provide a full oven atmosphere of steam, well before putting in the loaves. Top up the water when you put the loaves in.

Bake the loaves for about 30 min; after 15 min, open the oven door to let the steam escape, and remove the pans of water. Bake for the remainder of the time without steam, as this gives a crisp crust.

Cool the baked loaves on a cloth-covered tray.

5 loaves

VIENNESE BREAD ROLLS

Made like Viennese Bread but shape dough into rolls weighing about 2 oz each. Bake for 15–18 min, removing the pans of water after 8 min.

WHOLEMEAL ROLLS

Use the same ingredients as for Wholemeal Bread. Make the dough in the same way. After kneading, shape the dough into small rolls like the Fancy Bread Rolls, and leave them to prove on a lightly floured baking sheet, for 20–30 min. Bake for about 15 min at 200 °C, 425 °F, Gas 7.

WHOLEMEAL BREAD

3½ lb wholemeal flour	1 oz yeast
3½ teasp salt	2 oz lard
1 teasp sugar	1¾ pt warm water

Mix salt well with flour and make warm in a large basin. Cream the yeast with the sugar, add the warm water, together with the melted fat, and mix with the flour to an elastic dough. Knead well until smooth, cover with a cloth, to prevent surface evaporation, and set in a warm place to rise to double its size—about 1 hr. When the dough is sufficiently risen it has a honey-combed appearance. The first kneading distributes the yeast and softens the gluten of the flour. Knead the dough a second time to distribute the carbonic acid gas which has formed. Continue kneading until, when the dough is cut, there are no large holes in it, but do not knead too heavily. Divide into the number of loaves required. Place in warmed greased tins, making the top round. Prick and allow to prove or recover for 20 min or just until the dough is well up to the top of the tin and no longer. Bake in the middle of a very hot oven (230 °C, 450 °F, Gas 8) for 10–15 min, then reduce heat to fairly hot (190 °C, 375 °F,

Gas 5), baking in all about 1 hr. When ready the loaf should have a hollow sound when knocked on the bottom, and should be well risen and nicely browned with a crisp crust.

4 loaves　　　　　　　　*Cooking time 1 hr*

GOOD DRINKS WITH FONDUES

Tea is the classic Swiss drink with cheese fondues. It is usually served without milk or lemon. But you can serve it 'white' and sugared if you wish.

A liqueur-glass of kirsch half-way through the meal, say when a second pot of fondue is being prepared, makes a welcome break.

With meat, seafood and vegetable fondues, serve one of the hot or chilled drinks suggested at the beginning of this chapter. Remember that desserts need a sweet wine, as a rule.

End the meal with tea or coffee.

TEA, TO MAKE

Do not boil the water until you want to make the tea. Warm the pot by pouring in a little boiling water, then tipping it out. Use the amount of tea per person which you happen to like; the quantity may vary with the type of tea. Pour the boiling water on the tea.

Do not let the tea stand for more than 3–4 minutes before pouring it out.

MULLED WINE

½ pt water	½ lemon
6 cloves	1½ pt port *or*
¼ oz bruised cinnamon	claret
Nutmeg	Sugar

Put the water in an enamel saucepan and heat gently, stir in the cloves, cinnamon, a grate of nutmeg and the thinly-peeled rind of the lemon. Bring to the boil and cook for 10 min. Strain off the liquid into a basin and add the wine. Sweeten to taste. Return the liquid to the pan and make hot without boiling.

NEGUS

3 oz loaf sugar	¼ small nutmeg
1 lemon	2–3 drops
1 pt port	vanilla
1 pt boiling	essence
water	

Rub the sugar on the rind of the lemon until all the zest is extracted. Crush it in a basin and pour over it the port and boiling water. Add the nutmeg and the vanilla. Serve hot.

MULLED ALE

1 qt ale	Pinch of ground
1 tablesp castor	nutmeg
sugar	Good pinch of
Pinch of ground	ground ginger
cloves	1 glass rum *or*
	brandy

Put the ale, sugar, cloves, nutmeg and ginger into a stewpan, and bring nearly to boiling-point. Add the brandy and more sugar and flavouring if necessary; serve at once.

ALE JINGLE

1 roasted apple	Hot ale
2 slices plum	Nutmeg
cake	Sugar

Put the roasted apple and plum cake into a pint jug. Pour in sufficient hot ale almost to fill the jug. Add grated nutmeg and sugar to taste.

Serve at once.

TABLE WINES

Most people only buy wine when they need it, often just a few hours before drinking it. This is a bad practice if it can be avoided. You cannot always get the wine you want at such short notice. There is not usually enough time to acclimatize the wine to the room conditions and right drinking temperature. You often pay more for the wine than you need.

STORING TIME

If you can buy young wine a few years ahead of its best drinking time and store it, it may cost only half what it does when mature. This is not difficult to do. Many good wine merchants and wine clubs offer young wines 'for laying down', and the process of doing this is not nearly as difficult as it sounds.

You can, of course, hire space in a wine merchant's or club's to store your wine in. But for most people it is hardly worth doing. Any dark place at a temperature of about 60° will do, provided the temperature is fairly constant, the air is reasonably dry, and the wine can stay undisturbed. A loft or cellar, or the back of a cupboard under the stairs, are all suitable places.

Store the wine in racks with the labels upwards, so that you can see them easily. Keep a list of what wines you have, where they are, and when they should be drunk. Then stop worrying about them until you want to drink them.

DECANTING WINE

Ordinary table wines need not be decanted although most wine looks more attractive in clear glass and tastes better for the opportunity to 'breathe'.

The only wines you *must* decant are very good old wines such as vintage or crusted port and old burgundies and clarets which 'throw a sediment'. The decanter must be absolutely clean and dry and should not, under any circumstances, be washed in detergent. Stand the bottle up twenty-four hours before decanting to allow the sediment to fall to the bottom; otherwise place the bottle gently in a cradle from which it can be uncorked and decanted.

Having removed the cork, one hour before serving, clean the neck of the bottle inside and out with a damp clean cloth and make sure that the wine will not pour over any of the metal foil round the neck of the bottle. Gently lift the bottle and pour the wine steadily into the decanter, having first placed a candle or torch close to the shoulder of the bottle which will enable you to see the sediment and to know when to stop.

Both decanters and glasses should be as plain as possible and uncoloured.

Fewer types of glasses are used now than in the past. Champagne 'saucers' are now not thought a good way to serve champagne, as tall 'flutes' hold the bouquet better. For ordinary table wines, many people like to have one size and style of glass only, often a classic wine-tasting shape and type, instead of having larger glasses for white wines. Hocks and moselles, however, often gain from being drunk in the special, very graceful glasses, designed for them, but remember that coloured glass detracts from the colour of the wine.

Brandy 'balloons' are also going out as unpractical. Almost any thin glass tapering towards the top is now thought suitable. Similar glasses in the appropriate sizes are also thought best for port and sherry.

AFTER THE FONDUE

DESSERT—FRESH FRUIT

Make sure that all fresh fruit is well washed, dried and polished. Serve it in an attractive pattern on a tray, on a stemmed dish lined with green leaves, or in a sparklingly clean, plain glass bowl. Give each diner a clean plate and napkin, and a fruit knife and fork, preferably of silver.

Finger-bowls are a pleasant idea which are being revived now after a time in disfavour. They can be of silver, china or glass, and the clear water can contain a few drops of lemon juice or rose-water if you like.

BLACKCURRANT OR OTHER FRUIT WHIP

¼ pt blackcurrant purée (*see* **Fruit Purée**) and ½ pt water *or* ¾ pt	blackcurrant juice ½ oz gelatine Sugar to taste

Heat the gelatine slowly in the juice *or* purée and water until dissolved. Add sugar if necessary. Cool, then whisk briskly until a thick foam is produced. When the whisk leaves a trail in the foam, pile quickly into a glass dish.

Fruit flan

Damson Whip Use ¾ pt damson juice, ½ oz gelatine and sugar to taste.

Lemon Whip Use 1 pt lemon jelly tablet, sugar, ¾ pt water and 1 tablesp lemon juice.

Pineapple Whip Like Damson Whip.

Orange Whip Like Lemon Whip, using orange instead of lemon juice.

6 helpings   *Time ½ hr*

FRUIT FLAN OR TART (*cont. p. 54*)

Rich shortcrust pastry using 4 oz flour, etc.

Filling

1 medium-sized can of fruit *or* **¾ lb fresh fruit, e.g. apples, strawberrries, pears, pineapple, cherries, apricots, peaches, plums, etc. or dried fruit such as apple slices, apricots and prunes, well soaked**

Coating glaze

¼ pt syrup from canned fruit, *or* **fruit juice,** *or* **water**	**1 teasp arrowroot**
	Lemon juice to taste
Sugar (if necessary)	

Decoration (optional)

Whipped sweetened cream

Line a 7-in flan ring or tart plate with the pastry. Prick the bottom and bake it 'blind'. Bake for about 20 min first in a fairly hot oven (200 °C, 400 °F, Gas 6), then reducing the heat as the pastry sets to moderate (180 °C, 350 °F, Gas 4). When the pastry is cooked, remove the paper and filling used for 'blind' baking and replace the case in the oven for 5 min to dry the bottom. Allow to cool.

If fresh or dried fruit is used, stew gently till tender, if necessary. Drain the fruit. Place the sugar if used and the liquid in a pan and boil for 10 min. Blend the arrowroot with some lemon juice and add it to the syrup, stirring all the time. Continue stirring, cook for 3 min then cool slightly. Arrange the fruit attractively in the flan case and coat it with fruit syrup. Serve cold.

If liked, a flan can be decorated with piped whipped, sweetened cream.

For a quick flan or tart case, a crumb crust or cake mixture from a packet can be used satisfactorily.

In some areas, apple flans or tarts are given a crumbled cheese topping instead of fruit syrup.

FRUIT PURÉES

Fruit purées for all sweet dishes including creams, ice creams and sauces are made by rubbing fresh, frozen or canned fruit through a fine sieve, or by using an electric blender. Fruit containing pips or stones must be sieved before blending. A nylon sieve should always be used as fruit is acid.

FRUIT SALAD

3 oz granulated sugar	**6 oz green grapes**
½ pt water	**1 small can pineapple segments**
3 oranges	
Rind and juice of 1 lemon	**3 red-skinned dessert apples**
3 ripe dessert pears	

Bring the sugar and water to the boil, together with strips of rind taken from 1 orange and the lemon. Cool. Sieve to remove the rind.

Cut up the oranges, removing the skin and white pith, and section out the flesh, removing the pips. Halve the grapes removing the pips. Place these in the cooled sugar and water. Empty the pineapple pieces and juice into the fruit salad. Refrigerate if possible.

Just before serving, quarter, core and slice the apples thinly and toss in the lemon juice. Dice the pears and toss in lemon juice also. Add these to the fruit salad. Arrange attractively in a suitable serving dish. Chill and serve.

Fresh pineapple and canned mandarin segments are attractively coloured fruit to use. Try piling the salad in a shell or half shell of pineapple.

LEMON JELLY

4 lemons	**1 in cinnamon stick**
Sherry (optional)	
1½ pt water	**1¾–2 oz gelatine**
6 oz sugar	**Shells and whites of 2 eggs**
4 cloves	

Scald a large pan, whisk and metal jelly mould. Wash the lemons and cut thin strips of rind, omitting the white pith. Extract juice and measure. Make up to ½ pt with water *or* sherry, but do not add sherry until just before clearing the jelly. Put the 1½ pt water, ½ pt juice, rinds, sugar, flavourings and gelatine into the scalded pan and infuse, with a lid on, over very gentle heat until sugar and gelatine are dissolved. Do not let the infusion become hot. Wash egg-shells and crush. Lightly whisk the whites until liquid and add, with shells, to the infusion. Heat steadily, whisking constantly, until a good head of foam is produced, and the contents of the pan become hot, but not quite boiling. Strain through the crust as described above, and add the sherry, if used, as the jelly goes through the filter.

6 helpings   *Time 1–1½ hr*

LEMON MERINGUE PIE

Rich shortcrust pastry, using 8oz flour, etc.

Filling:

2 eggs	2 oz castor sugar
8 oz can sweetened condensed milk	2 level teasp cream of tartar
	1 lemon

Make the pastry and line an 8 or 9-in pie plate. Bake it 'blind'.

To make the filling Separate the egg yolks from the whites. Beat the yolks until thick and lemon coloured. Fold in the condensed milk, lemon rind, juice and cream of tartar. Pour into the baked pie shell. Spread with meringue made from the egg whites and the sugar. Decorate lightly with cherries and angelica. Bake in a cool oven (100 °C, 200 °F, Gas ½) for ½–1 hr.

LEMON OR ORANGE SORBET

1 pt water	½ pt lemon *or* orange juice
8 oz loaf sugar	
2 egg whites	

Dissolve the sugar in the water. Boil for 10 min, strain and cool. Add the juice and stiffly whisked egg whites. Freeze and serve at once.

6 helpings

LEMON WATER ICE

6 lemons	1½ pt syrup, as below
2 oranges	

Peel the fruit thinly and place the rind in a basin. Add the hot syrup, cover and cool. Add the juice of the lemons and oranges. Strain, chill and freeze.

Syrup for Water Ices

2 lb loaf sugar	1 pt water

Place the sugar and water in a strong saucepan. Allow the sugar to dissolve over gentle heat. Do not stir. When the sugar has dissolved, gently boil the mixture for 10 min, or, if a saccharometer is available, until it registers about 100 °C, 220 °F. Remove scum as it rises. Strain, cool and store. Makes 1 pt syrup.

6 helpings

MERINGUE FLAN WITH APPLE OR PEAR FILLING

Short crust pastry, frozen *or* using 4 oz flour, etc.	2 oz butter *or* margarine
	3 oz brown sugar
	2 eggs
1½ lb cooking apples *or* pears	2–3 oz castor sugar for the meringue
2 tablesp water	Marzipan apples *or* glacé cherries
Rind of ½ lemon	
1 pinch each ground cinnamon and cloves	

Peel, core and slice the apples or pears; put them in a saucepan and stew with the water and the finely-grated lemon rind. When soft, sieve or process in an electric blender. Return the pulp to the pan and re-heat slightly, add the butter, brown sugar and egg yolks. Meanwhile line a 7-in flan ring with the pastry. Put the fruit mixture into the uncooked lined flan ring and bake gently in a moderate oven (180 °C, 350 °F, Gas 4) for about 30 min, until the fruit mixture is set. Stiffly whisk the egg whites and fold in 2–3 oz castor sugar. Pile on top of the fruit mixture, dredge lightly with castor sugar and decorate, if you wish, with pieces of angelica and glacé cherry. Bake in a very cool oven (140 °C, 290 °F, Gas 1) until the meringue is golden-brown, about 30–40 min. Top with marzipan apples or glacé cherries before serving.

Meringue pie with apple filling

This recipe can also be used for tartlets, if the cooking time is reduced.

6–7 helpings

BASIC MILANAISE SOUFFLÉ

2 lemons	**½ oz gelatine**
3–4 eggs,	**¼ pt water**
** according to**	**½ pt double cream**
** size**	
5 oz castor sugar	

Decoration:
Chopped pistachio nuts

Wash lemons dry, and grate rind finely. Whisk the egg yolks, sugar, rind and lemon juice over hot water until thick and creamy, then remove bowl from the hot water and continue whisking until cool. Soften the gelatine in the ¼ pt water, and heat to dissolve. Half-whip the cream. Whisk the egg whites very stiffly. Add the gelatine, still hot, in a thin stream, to the egg mixture, and stir in as you do it. Fold in the cream and the stiffly-whipped whites. Fold the mixture very lightly until setting is imminent, when the mixture pulls against the spoon. Pour into the soufflé dish and leave to set. Remove the paper band by coaxing it away from the mixture with a knife dipped in hot water. Decorate the sides with chopped, blanched pistachio nuts, and the top with whipped cream, if liked.

This is a good 'basic' soufflé recipe. It can be flavoured and decorated with almost

Milanaise soufflé   Peach Condé

any flavouring and garnish, such as coffee, chocolate, fruit or a liqueur, with appropriate small sweets or nuts as decoration.

6 helpings   *Setting time 2 hr*

PEACH OR PEAR CONDÉ

1 pt cold rice mould	**1 level teasp arrowroot**
⅛ pt double cream	
Whipped cream	
1 small can peaches *or* pears	

Stir the cream into the rice. Pour into serving dishes. Drain the fruit and arrange it prettily on top.

Make the juice up to ¼ pt with water. Blend in the arrowroot, and boil until clear. Cool, then pour over the fruit. Decorate with whipped cream.

4 helpings

ORANGE FLUMMERY *(Method, p. 58)*

1st layer:

6 oz canned orange juice	**3 oz castor sugar**
1½ level teasp gelatine	**2 eggs, separated**
	Orange segments
1 oz castor sugar	**2 level tablesp cornflour**
	Angelica

2nd layer:

1 13½ oz can orange juice	**2 level teasp gelatine**

57

Make the first layer, by dissolving the gelatine in the orange juice, warmed. Add the sugar and dissolve without boiling. Pour this jelly into the base of a 2 pt mould. Chill to set it.

Make the second layer. Dissolve the gelatine in 4 oz of the juice, warmed. Leave to cool. Blend the cornflour with a little juice, dissolve the sugar by warming it in the rest of the juice, and pour it on the blended cornflour. When the mixture has cooled slightly, beat in the egg yolks. Stir in the dissolved gelatine, trickling it in from a height, and chill the mixture. When it begins to thicken, whisk the egg whites and fold them carefully into the mixture with a wooden spoon. Pour into the mould and leave to set. When the whole is set, turn out carefully, and decorate with orange segments and angelica.

PEACH MELBA

4-5 firm, ripe peaches	4 oz sugar
½ gill Melba sauce	½ pt vanilla ice cream, home-made *or* bought
Vanilla essence	

Halve and peel the peaches. Add the vanilla to the syrup and dissolve in it the sugar. Poach the peaches in the syrup until tender but not broken. Lift out the peaches, drain them on a sieve, and allow to get thoroughly cold. Serve them piled around a mound of vanilla ice cream in a silver dish. Set this dish in another dish containing shaved ice. Pour over a rich raspberry syrup, which must be previously iced. Serve at once.

This is the original recipe created in honour of Dame Nellie Melba. It is now often made as follows:

1 pt vanilla ice cream	½ pt Melba sauce
6 canned peach halves	¼ pt sweetened whipped cream

Place a scoop or slice of ice cream in 6 sundae glasses. Cover with a peach half. Coat with Melba sauce. Pipe a large rose of cream on top of each.

Other fruits are also used. Pears dipped in lemon juice team well with raspberries, for instance.

6 individual glasses

Melba Sauce

To make Melba sauce pass the required quantity of fresh raspberries through a nylon sieve and sweeten with icing sugar. The sauce is not cooked. Use as required.

STRAWBERRY SHORTCAKE

8 oz plain flour	½ oz grounds almonds
⅛ teasp salt	
Pinch of baking powder	4½ oz margarine
	2 oz sugar
	1 egg yolk

Filling:

1 pt strawberries	1–2 gills whipped cream
Sugar to taste	

Sift flour, salt and baking powder and mix with the ground almonds. Cream the fat and sugar and add egg yolk. Work in the flour mixture as for a cake of shortbread. Divide into three pieces and roll into rounds a good ¼-in thick. Bake in a moderate oven (180 °C, 350 °F, Gas 4) until golden-brown, then allow to become cold. Crush strawberries slightly with sugar to taste and add a little whipped cream. Spread this on to the first round of shortcake, cover with the second round and so on, finishing with a layer of strawberries. Pipe whipped cream on top and round the edges. Decorate as desired.

1 Self-raising flour can be used, without the baking powder.

2 Pears make a good addition to the strawberries. Slice the peeled pears, poach them and drain well before using.

Cooking time 30–40 min

COFFEE, TO MAKE

You need large cups of coffee after a fondue. 'Instant' coffee can be used, but freshly-roasted and ground coffee is much better. Good coffee shops roast their coffee daily, and will grind it for you to the fineness you want, if you have no coffee-grinder of your own.

If you buy ground coffee, only buy a small quantity at a time, and keep it in an air-tight container. It loses its aroma and flavour very quickly.

Most people have their own favourite way of making coffee. Use the one you prefer. You can make it like tea, with a pinch of salt added, and strain it; or you can use one of the various kinds of percolator or vacuum jug.

Don't serve a *café filtre* or *espresso coffee* with a fondue. They are strong, and are meant to be served in small cups after a more formal dinner.

Meat Casseroles

CASSEROLES ARE labour-saving from first to last. They can cook, without attention, either in the oven or on top of the stove. Since they usually contain vegetables, either as a mirepoix or separate, larger pieces, they save dishes and make little washing-up. Many can be cooked overnight at a very low heat, simply being reheated when wanted for use. So they are a boon to the busy or working house-wife.

Casseroles have other advantages in that they often make use of cheap ingredients, yet feed a hungry family with nourishing food more than adequately.

We include, in the following sections, the oven-cooked dishes which Americans call 'bakes' and which they have made particularly their own. These usually include some form of starch such as *pasta*, and many are 'finished' or garnished with attractive savoury toppings. They are adaptable and convenient dishes. Many use packaged or 'instant' products; and simply by reducing or increasing the amounts of the various ingredients, one can make them suitable for one person or for serving a crowd.

Beef Creole

Beef olives

Both casseroles and 'bakes' are versatile in another way too. Whether savoury or sweet, the ingredients can usually be varied to suit the housewife's particular needs or the goods in her store-cupboard. They are truly all-purpose, 'any-time' dishes.

BEEF À LA MODE

2 lb rump of beef	1 oz butter *or* fat
1 glass claret	10 button onions
Juice of ½ lemon	1 oz flour
1 small onion	1½ pt stock
2 cloves	2 bacon rashers
Salt and pepper	2 carrots
Bouquet garni	

Trim and bone the meat. Place it in a bowl with a marinade made from the claret, lemon juice, finely-chopped onion, cloves, salt, pepper and bouquet garni. Leave for 2 hr, basting frequently. Melt the fat in a stewpan, drain the beef well and fry until brown. Fry the button onions at the same time. Remove both from the pan, add the flour and fry until nut-brown. Then add the stock and the marinade in which the meat was soaked and stir until boiling. Replace the meat and the onions and season to taste. Cover the meat with the bacon rashers. Add the carrots, thinly sliced, and cook gently for 2½ hr, stirring occasionally. When tender, place on a hot dish, strain the liquid in the saucepan and pour over the meat.

8 helpings

BEEF CREOLE *(Method, p. 62)*

2 lb beef cut in cubes	2 lb onions
1 teasp salt	2 lb fresh tomatoes
1 teasp pepper	1 pepper
3 rashers fat bacon	

Season the meat. Place on the rashers of bacon in an earthenware casserole. Cover with sliced onions, tomatoes and pepper. Simmer slowly until beef is tender, the time depending on the cut used.

6 helpings

BEEF OLIVES

1½ lb stewing steak	Salt and pepper to taste
2 oz fresh white breadcrumbs	1 egg
1 rounded tablesp dried skim milk powder	1 oz plain flour
	2 oz dripping
4 level tablesp chopped suet	½ lb onions, peeled and sliced
2 level tablesp chopped parsley	1 pt stock
A good pinch of dried herbs	1 pt pkt dehydrated 'instant' potato
Grated rind of ½ lemon	½ teasp ground nutmeg

Remove any excess fat from the meat and cut it into 12 even-sized pieces. For the stuffing, mix together the breadcrumbs, dry milk powder, suet, parsley, herbs, lemon rind and seasoning. Stir in the egg with a little more milk powder made into liquid if necessary. Use just enough to bind the mixture lightly together. Divide the stuffing between the pieces of meat and roll into neat rolls. Wind a piece of cotton round the meat or use a wooden cocktail skewer, to keep the stuffing in place. Add a little seasoning to the flour and roll the meat in it. Heat the dripping in a heat-proof casserole or pan and fry the meat until browned all over. Carefully lift out the meat. Fry the onions and carrots until lightly browned, then return the meat to the casserole, with any remaining flour. Pour over the stock and bring slowly to the boil. Put a lid on the pan or casserole and simmer for about 1½ hr until the meat is tender. The beef olives can also be cooked in a slow oven (150 °C, 310 °F, Gas 2), for about 2½ hr.

6 helpings

CARBONNADE OF BEEF

1½ lb good stewing steak	½ pt beer
2 oz dripping	Salt and pepper
2 large onions, sliced	6 thin rounds of bread
1 clove of garlic	Mustard and vinegar *or*
½ oz flour	French mustard
½ pt stock *or* water	

Wipe and trim the meat, removing all fat and cut into 1½ in squares. Heat the dripping in a stewpan and brown the meat quickly on all sides. Add the sliced onions and fry until brown. Add the crushed garlic and fry lightly. Pour off the surplus fat, sprinkle in the flour and brown slightly. Add the stock or water, beer and seasoning. Place in a casserole and cook gently in a warm oven (170 °C, 335 °F, Gas 3) for 1½–2 hr. When cooked, spread the rounds of bread with mustard and vinegar or French mustard, and press well down into the gravy. Return the casserole to the oven for about 15 min without the lid and allow the bread to brown slightly. Serve in the casserole.

6 helpings

ESTOUFFADE OF BEEF

4–5 lb top rump or topside	Brandy
Dripping	Bouquet garni
2 carrots	Bay leaf
3 onions, peeled and cut in rings	1 lb streaky bacon in one piece
½ bottle white wine	

Trim the beef. Melt the dripping in a deep flame-proof casserole with a tight-fitting lid. Put in the meat, carrots and onion rings. Cook over a gentle flame for about 15 min. Add the wine, and a little brandy if you wish, the bouquet, bay leaf, and the bacon cut into dice. Cover the casserole, place it in the oven at the lowest possible heat, about 110 °C, 220 °F, Gas Mark 'Warm', and leave for 7–8 hours or overnight. Serve with mashed or creamed potatoes.

This is one of the classic dishes which the French developed long ago to follow a fast-day or church-going day such as Christmas Eve. It can cook all night (or all day while the family is at church or occupied) and is spoon-tender ready when they want it on the following evening. It is a favourite dish for the night before Christmas Day. The long slow cooking gives it a rich, aromatic sauce, and the wine and brandy lift it into the luxury class.

6–8 helpings

SPICY GOULASCH

1 lb chuck steak	1 clove garlic,
1 oz flour,	peeled
seasoned	2 tablesp paprika
1 oz lard or hard	¼ teasp Tabasco
dripping	sauce
1 large onion,	1 pt beef stock *or*
peeled	bouillon

Cut the steak into 1-in cubes. Coat with the flour. Melt the fat in a flameproof casserole. Slice the onion.

Sauté the onion until golden-brown. Remove from the casserole, and brown the meat on all sides. Add the onions, the garlic clove, paprika and Tabasco sauce, and gradually pour in the stock or bouillon. Cook at 180 °C, 350 °F, Gas Mark 4 for 1–1¼ hr, until the meat is tender.

3–4 helpings

LAMB CUTLETS, CASSEROLED

6–8 lamb cutlets	1 lb canned
2 tablesp cooking	young carrots
oil	1 lb canned new
1 teasp Tabasco	potatoes
sauce	2 meat extract
Salt and freshly-	cubes
ground black	2 pts water
pepper	Chopped parsley
½ lb frozen	to garnish
garden peas	

Brown the cutlets in the oil, on both sides. While they cook, sprinkle them with the Tabasco sauce, salt and pepper.

Mix the peas, carrots and potatoes in a casserole. Add the cutlets. Add any remaining meat juices and fat from the frying pan. Stir in the stock. Cover and cook in the oven at 180 °C, 350 °F, Gas Mark 4, for 30–45 min, until cutlets are tender. Garnish with parsley.

3–4 helpings

BRAISED BREAST OF LAMB

A breast of lamb	**Salt and pepper**

Mirepoix:

2 onions	2 or 3 potatoes
2 carrots	(optional)
2 sticks celery	1 or 2 sliced
½ turnip	tomatoes
½ oz dripping	(optional)
1 oz fat bacon	Chopped spinach
Bouquet garni	Stock

Braise the breast of lamb as follows: bone the meat and season well with salt and pepper. Roll tightly and secure with string. Prepare the mirepoix by cutting the onions, carrots, celery and turnip into thick pieces. Melt the dripping in a flame-proof casserole and gently fry the vege-tables with the fat bacon with the lid on the pan for 10 min. Add the bouquet garni, the potatoes and tomatoes (if used) and suffi-cient stock to almost cover the vegetables. Bring to the boil. Place the meat on top of the mirepoix, cover with the casserole lid. Cook slowly for about 2 hr until meat is tender. Baste frequently.

5–6 helpings

NAVARIN OF LAMB *(Method, p. 66)*

1 large breast *or*	8–10 small onions
boned neck of	8–10 small
lamb	potatoes
A good pinch of	10 oz peas,
sugar	frozen,
1 large tablesp	dehydrated *or*
flour	canned
½ lb skinned	(optional)
tomatoes	10 oz small
1 crushed clove	whole carrots,
of garlic	frozen *or* canned
Salt and pepper	(optional)
Bouquet garni	Chopped parsley

▲ Estouffade of Beef

opposite page top Midsummer Lamb Casserole and Golden Harvest Chicken Casserole

opposite page left Braised lamb with Paprika

opposite page right Boston pork casserole

Spicy Goulasch

Cut the lamb in neat slices, having trimmed off tag ends and excess fat. Chop the fat and heat it gently. Fry the meat pieces in some of it, then transfer them to a casserole. Pour off the fat. Sprinkle the sugar into the pan and heat until it becomes a deep gold. Work in the flour and then the chopped tomatoes (seeds discarded), then stir in enough hot water to make a sauce to cover the meat. Pour over the meat. Add the crushed garlic, a little pepper and salt and the bouquet garni. Cover, cook for $1\frac{1}{2}$ hr first in a moderate oven ($180\,^{\circ}$C, $350\,^{\circ}$F, Gas 4) reducing to $150\,^{\circ}$C, $310\,^{\circ}$F, Gas 2 after $\frac{1}{2}$ hr. Remove bouquet garni; add the onions and potatoes, turn up the heat to $180\,^{\circ}$C, $350\,^{\circ}$F, Gas 4 and cook for a further $\frac{1}{2}-\frac{3}{4}$ hr. Add the drained, cooked peas and carrots if used, and heat through. Sprinkle with parsley and serve.

6 helpings

IRISH STEW

2 lb best end of neck of lamb	3 lb potatoes
1 lb onions	$1\frac{1}{2}$ pt stock *or* water
Salt and pepper	Parsley

Cut the meat into neat pieces and trim off the surplus fat. Arrange in a saucepan layers of the meat, thinly sliced onions, seasoning and $\frac{1}{2}$ the potatoes cut in slices. Add stock or water just to cover and simmer gently for about $1\frac{1}{2}$ hr. Add the rest of the potatoes, cut to a uniform size to improve the appearance on top. Cook gently in the steam for about $\frac{3}{4}$ hr longer. Serve the meat in the centre of a hot dish and arrange the potatoes round the edge. Pour the liquid over the meat and sprinkle with finely-chopped parsley.

6 helpings

CASSEROLE OF COOKED LAMB

2 lb cold cooked lean lamb	Salt and pepper
2 lb potatoes	$\frac{3}{4}$ pt gravy from the meat trimmings
2 onions	

Cut the meat into neat thin pieces. Make the gravy. Parboil and slice the potatoes and onions. Line a pie dish with slices of potato and cover with layers of meat, onions and potatoes, seasoning each layer. Repeat in layers until all the ingredients are used; the top layer should consist of potato. Add the gravy, cover with the greaseproof paper and bake in a moderate oven ($180\,^{\circ}$C, $250\,^{\circ}$F, Gas 4) for 1 hr. For the last 15 min remove the greaseproof paper to allow the potatoes to brown.

6 helpings

MIDSUMMER LAMB CASSEROLE

1 oz butter	$\frac{3}{4}$ pint mixed light stock and dry cider (half and half)
1 onion, sliced	
8 oz carrots, peeled and sliced	
1 medium-sized turnip, peeled and diced	$\frac{1}{4}$ level teasp dried marjoram
	Salt and pepper
4 oz button mushrooms, halved	2 teasp single cream
1 oz plain flour	Chopped parsley

Melt the butter in a flameproof casserole. Add the onion, carrots and turnips and cook for 2–3 min. Add the mushrooms and lamb, and cook one min longer. Stir in the flour, and cook for 1 min. Gradually, stir in the stock and cider. Bring to the boil, still stirring. Add the marjoram and seasoning. Cover, and simmer gently for $\frac{3}{4}$–1 hr, or until the lamb and vegetables are tender. Just before serving, stir in the cream, and garnish with chopped parsley.

4 helpings

PORK CHOPS WITH RED CABBAGE

$\frac{1}{2}$ medium-sized head red cabbage, shredded	3 tablesp chopped parsley
	$\frac{1}{2}$ pt vegetable *or* chicken stock
4 thick pork chops	1 teasp lemon juice
1 tablesp butter	1 egg yolk
15 chestnuts, peeled	Salt

Blanch the cabbage. Brown the chops on

66

both sides in the butter. Grease a deep casserole and preheat the oven to 180 °C, 350 °F, Gas Mark 4.

Place the cabbage in the casserole, and pour over any fat remaining from browning the chops. Arrange the chestnuts in a layer on the cabbage. Place the chops on top. Pour in the stock. Cover, and cook in the oven for 1½ hr or longer if necessary, until the chops and cabbage are tender, and the chestnuts cooked through. Add more stock if needed.

Just before serving, mix the lemon juice, egg yolk and a good pinch of salt. Mix in 1 tablesp juice from the casserole. Pour the mixture back into the casserole slowly, stirring it in.

4 helpings

BOSTON PORK CASSEROLE

1 lb dried haricot beans	4 tablesp black treacle
2 medium onions, peeled and thinly sliced	2 level teasp dry mustard
	1 level teasp salt
½–¾ lb fat belly of salt pork cut into 1-in cubes	Good shake pepper

Wash the beans, cover with water and leave to soak overnight. Drain but keep ½ pt water. Fill a large heat-proof casserole (or traditional bean pot) with beans, onions and pork. Combine the reserved water with the remaining ingredients, pour into casserole, then cover with lid. Cook in the centre of a very slow oven (140 °C, 290 °F, Gas 1) for 5–6 hr. Stir occasionally and add a little more water if beans seem to dry slightly while cooking.

4 helpings

LOIN OF VEAL, DAUBE STYLE

A small shoulder of veal	1 turnip
Salt and pepper	2 stalks celery
2 oz dripping	Bouquet garni
2 onions	Stock as required
	Piquant sauce

Stuffing:

½ large onion	Parsley
1 oz butter	2 egg yolks
3 stalks celery	3–4 oz white breadcrumbs
2 eating apples	Stock
1 oz walnuts, chopped	

Bone the veal, flatten it out and season well with salt and pepper. Roll up and tie with string. Sauté in hot fat until brown on all sides and remove. Peel the onions, carrots, turnips; clean the celery, chop coarsely; fry all the vegetables in dripping until just turning colour. Make a mound of the sautéed vegetables in centre of casserole. Place veal on top, add the bouquet garni and sufficient stock to cover the vegetables and braise with lid on until meat is tender.

Stuffing Peel and slice the onion; fry in butter until soft. Add the finely diced celery and apples, walnuts and parsley and egg yolks and sufficient breadcrumbs to make a soft stuffing. Simmer, moistening with stock when necessary, for 15 min.

Serve veal on a bed of the vegetables with the stuffing arranged at each end of the veal, and serve Piquant sauce separately.

CASSEROLED VEAL WITH PEAS AND PEPPERS

1½ lb boneless veal, cut from the leg	¾ pint chicken bouillon or broth
1 tablesp olive oil	½ gill white wine
4 oz uncooked long grain rice	Grated peel of ½ lemon
½ oz butter	2 oz button mushrooms, halved
4 oz green peas, fresh or frozen	Beurre manié
2 green and 2 red bell peppers, deseeded	Chopped parsley

Cut the veal into ¾-in cubes. Sauté briefly in the oil in a flame-proof casserole, then leave aside. Discard any poor-quality fresh peas; thaw frozen ones. Cut the peppers into chunks.

Remove the veal from the casserole. Add the rice and butter to the oil. Heat just enough to melt the butter. Replace the

left Loin of Veal, Daube style

top right Beef, apples, carrots and onions in a classic casserole

bottom right Lamb with fresh apples and tomatoes

opposite page Lamb chops 'en casserole'

veal and add the peas and peppers. Mix bouillon, wine, grated lemon peel together, and pour over the vegetables. Season if required. Cover the casserole, and cook in a moderate oven, 180 °C, 350 °F, Gas Mark 4, for 50 min or until veal is tender.

Drain the sauce from the casserole into a small saucepan. Top the casserole vegetables with the mushrooms.

Bring the sauce to the boil, and simmer for about 10 min to reduce it slightly. Add enough beurre manié in small pieces to thicken the sauce to your taste. Pour the thickened sauce over the contents of the casserole. Cover again, and let the casserole bake in the oven for a further 15 min, to cook the mushrooms and become thoroughly hot. Top with the parsley just before serving.

4 helpings

BRAISED CHILLED LAMB WITH PAPRIKA

2 lb middle neck chilled or frozen lamb, chopped	1 dessertsp paprika
2 oz dripping	1 8-oz can tomatoes
8 oz onions, peeled and chopped	½ pt chicken bouillon or stock
1 clove garlic, crushed	4 oz green beans, fresh or frozen
1 dessertsp dried mixed peppers (optional)	Salt and pepper

Fry the lamb cutlets in the hot fat for 3–4 min, turning to brown all sides. Drain and place in a 3–4 pt casserole. Fry the onions and garlic slowly in the remaining fat until soft but not brown; add the peppers if used, and fry for a further 2–3 min; stir in the paprika and add the tomatoes and stock. Bring this sauce to the boil and pour over the cutlets. Bake, uncovered in a moderate oven (180°C, 350°F, Gas 4) for 1¾ hr. Garnish with green beans before serving.

POT PIE OF VEAL

1¼ lb lean veal	1 lb potatoes
¼ pickled pork	Puff pastry using 6 oz flour, etc.
Salt and pepper	
Stock	

Cut the meat into pieces convenient for serving and cut the pork into thin small slices. Place the meat and pork in layers in a large casserole, seasoning each layer well with salt and pepper, and fill the dish ¾ full with stock. Cover with a lid and cook in a moderate oven (180°C, 350°F, Gas 4) for 1½ hr. Meanwhile parboil the potatoes and cut in thick slices. After cooking for 1½ hr, allow the meat to cool slightly. Add more stock if necessary, place the potatoes on top, cover with pastry and make a hole in the top. Bake in a very hot oven (230°C, 450°F, Gas 8) until the pastry is set, reduce heat and cook more slowly for the remainder of the time, making 40–50 min altogether. Add more hot stock through the hole in the top before serving. Garnish with parsley and serve.

6 helpings

CASSEROLED LAMBS' HEARTS

6 lambs' hearts	2 oz dripping
Mixed chopped parsley and butter or minced bacon	½ pt good stock
	¾ oz flour
	Salt and pepper

Soak the hearts for about ½ hr. Wash well in clean water. Cut the pipes from the top, leave the flaps to fasten down and cut the dividing walls of the chambers. Dry thoroughly and fill the hearts with force-meat or parsley mixture, fold over the flaps and tie or skewer to keep it in. Heat the dripping in a casserole. Put in the hearts, baste well and bake in a cool to moderate oven (150°–180°C, 310°–350°F, Gas 2–4) for 1½ hr. When cooked, place the hearts on a hot dish and keep hot. Drain off most of the fat but keep back any sediment. Blend the flour and stock and add to the sediment to make thickened gravy. Season carefully. Pour a little round the hearts and serve the rest in a gravy-boat.

Sheeps' hearts can also be stuffed with sage and onion stuffing.

6 helpings

KIDNEY HOT POT

1 lb ox kidney	Salt and pepper
¼ lb lean bacon rashers	Stock
2 large onions	1½ lb potatoes
3 tomatoes	Bacon fat
3 oz mushrooms	Parsley

Soak the kidney in salt water for 15 min. Wash well, skin if necessary, remove the core and any fat and cut the kidney into slices about ¼ in. thick. Cut the bacon into pieces and the onions, tomatoes and mushrooms into slices. Put alternate slices of kidney, bacon, onion, tomatoes and mushrooms in a casserole, seasoning each layer. Three-quarters fill the casserole with stock and cover the top with a thick layer of sliced potatoes. Place some bacon rinds on top. Cover and cook at 180°C, 350°F, Gas 4 for 2½ hr. Remove the lid and bacon rinds ½ hr before serving. Dot the top with small pieces of bacon fat and allow the potatoes to brown. Sprinkle with finely chopped parsley.

6 helpings

OX TAIL STEW

2 ox tails	Salt and pepper
2 oz fat	Bouquet garni
2 onions	Cloves to taste
1½ oz flour	Mace to taste
1½ pt stock *or* water	Juice of ½ lemon

Garnish:

Croûtons of fried bread	Diced *or* glazed strips of carrot and turnip

Wash the tails, dry well and remove any superfluous fat. Cut into joints and divide the thick parts in half. Melt the fat in a saucepan, fry the pieces of tail until brown, then remove from the pan. Slice the onions and fry them until light brown, add the flour, mix well and fry slowly until a good brown colour. Add the stock or water, salt, pepper, bouquet garni, cloves and mace and bring to boiling-point, stirring all the time. Return the pieces of tail and simmer gently for about 2½–3 hr. Remove the meat and arrange on a hot dish. Add the lemon juice to the sauce, correct the seasoning, strain and pour over the meat. Garnish with croûtons of fried bread and diced or thin strips of cooked carrot and turnip.

6 helpings

MEAT CASSEROLES WITH FRUIT

The Middle East in particular is famed for its rich, redolent dishes in which fruit is mixed with the meat. The old, courtly cuisine of Iran, once Persia, is full of them. Here are a few from there and elsewhere in the area, together with some surprising additions from our own traditional fare.

BEEF STEW WITH APPLES

2 lb top rump of beef	2 cloves garlic, peeled
2 onions	Bouquet garni
2 carrots	¼ pt beef stock *or* bouillon
1 oz seasoned flour	⅛ pt white wine
2 tablesp olive oil	1 eating apple, dipped in lemon juice
3–4 oz bacon, diced	

Cut the meat into 1-in cubes, peel and quarter the onions and scrape the carrots. Toss in the flour. Fry the bacon lightly in a deep, flameproof casserole, add and heat the oil; then fry the meat and vegetables gently until beginning to colour. Remove from the heat.

Bury the garlic cloves and bouquet among the ingredients in the casserole. Pour in the stock or bouillon and the wine. Cover and bring to the boil. Lower the heat and simmer gently for 2–2½ hr until the meat is very tender.

Just before serving, cut the apple into pieces, and add to the casserole.

ARABIAN LAMB WITH APRICOTS

2 oz margarine	2 tablesp raisins
1 onion, finely chopped	4 oz dried apricots, soaked and halved
1½ lb lamb	1 lb uncooked rice
Salt and freshly-ground black pepper	
½ teasp ground cinnamon	

Heat the margarine gently in a flameproof casserole, and fry the onion until tender and golden. Trim the meat of fat, and cut it into 1-in cubes. Add it to the onion, and brown the pieces all over in the fat. Sprinkle with the seasonings. Add the raisins and drained apricots, and toss in the fat for 1–2 min until well coated.

Add enough water to cover the ingredients, bring almost to the boil, and simmer gently with a lid on the casserole for 1–1½ hr until the meat is tender. If desired, raise the heat and reduce the sauce by fast boiling at the end of the cooking, to give a stronger, thicker sauce.

While the meat cooks, boil the rice in salted, fast-boiling water for 10 min. Drain and rinse under the hot tap. Place in a shallow casserole with a clean cloth on top. Either place in the bottom of a heated oven for 30 min, or on top of the simmering stew. Either way, the damp rice 'steams' and the cloth absorbs the moisture.

Serve with salad.

4–5 helpings

Pork chops with apples and corn

opposite page top Casserole of veal with dumplings and apple garnish

opposite page bottom right Sausage casserole

bottom left Curried veal with fruit, raisins and rice

LAMB WITH FRESH APPLES AND TOMATOES

2 lb lean lamb, cubed
2 tablesp butter or oil
¼ lb yellow split peas
Salt and black pepper
1 lb sliced onions

1 apple, peeled, cored and diced
Lemon juice (optional)
2 tomatoes, quartered
Watercress to garnish

Turn the meat in hot butter or oil in a large saucepan until lightly coloured all over. Add the split peas and water to cover and season to taste with salt and black pepper. Add the onions. Bring to the boil and skim off any scum. Cover the pan and simmer for 2 hr, or until the meat is very tender.

Add the diced apple and quartered tomatoes and a little more water if necesary. Adjust seasoning. Cook for a few moments to heat the fruit through.

72

BEEF 'BAKE' WITH FRUIT

2 oz quick-cooking rolled oats	2 green or red bell peppers, seeded and chopped
1 tablesp dried onion flakes	
½ gill milk	4 oz mushrooms, sliced
1½ lb minced beef or beef and veal mixed	Salt and freshly-ground black pepper
2 eggs	
1 orange or tangerine, peeled and cut in skinless segments	Topping (see recipe)

Soak the oats and onion flakes in the milk until soft. Grease a shallow casserole. Mix all the ingredients, and spoon loosely into the casserole. Bake at 180 °C, 350 °F, Gas Mark 4, tightly covered. 15 min before the end of the cooking time, uncover and cover with one of the toppings in the last section if you wish.

4 helpings

LAMB CHOPS 'EN CASSEROLE'

4 thick loin lamb chops	¾ pint beef bouillon
Salt and pepper	⅛th pint white wine
1½ tablesp olive oil	
1 clove garlic, minced	Bouquet garni
	Flour if required
6–8 baby onions	Thin slices of apple, dipped in lemon juice
6 carrots, scraped and sliced	

Season the chops with salt and pepper, and sauté them briefly on both sides in the oil with the garlic and onions, peeled but whole. Add the carrots, and sauté for a few more minutes. Transfer the meat and vegetables to a well-greased deep casserole. Pour in the bouillon and wine, and add the bouquet garni. Cover tightly, and cook in the oven at 190 °C, 375F, Gas Mark 5 for 50–60 minutes or until the chops are tender and the vegetables cooked through. If a thick gravy is wanted, stir in a little flour mixed to a smooth, semi-liquid paste

with water. Just before serving, mix in the apple slices.

4 helpings

PORK CHOPS WITH APPLE AND CORN

1 oz butter	1½ oz flour
1 tablesp oil	A little dried majoram and thyme
4 pork chops	
1½ lb peeled potatoes	1 pt chicken stock
3 dessert apples, cored and sliced thickly	Parsley to garnish
3 corn cobs (canned) cut into pieces	

Melt the butter with the oil in a saucepan and in this sauté the chops, potatoes and apples until golden-brown, about 5–6 minutes. Add the corn pieces, flour and herbs. Finally, add the stock, cover and simmer for 25–30 min or until chops and potatoes are tender.

Serve hot, garnished with parsley.

BRAISED PORK CHOPS IN CIDER

4 pork chops	2–3 large dark mushrooms
4 tablesp cider	
Bouquet garni	1 breakfastcup or 10 oz can garden peas
3 onions	
2 cooking apples	
Good pinch of ground cinnamon	1 breakfastcup or 10 oz can beetroots
Salt and pepper	6–8 oz noodles

Trim off rind and excessive fat and quickly fry chops in them until golden brown. Place in a casserole, add cider and bouquet garni, cover and cook gently on the cooker or in a cool oven (150°–170°C, 310°–335°F, Gas 2–3). Meanwhile, pour off excess fat from frying-pan; peel, chop, then fry the onions and apples for a few minutes. Add the cinnamon and water to cover them, put on a lid and simmer until soft. Sieve, season to taste and turn on to the chops. Cover and cook for 1¾–2 hr in all, adding the thickly sliced mushrooms ½ hr before the end. Heat the peas and

74

beetroots separately. Trickle the noodles into salted boiling water and boil until, on testing a piece, the centre is still slightly firm (about 8 min). Drain the noodles, peas and beetroots. Dish the noodles with the chops on top and garnish with the mushrooms, peas and beetroots.

4 helpings

CASSEROLE OF VEAL WITH DUMPLINGS AND APPLE GARNISH

1½ lb lean stewing or pie veal	¼ pt white sauce
2 onions	Beurre manié
2 tablesp oil or lard	Salt and pepper
	Bouquet garni
1–2 cloves of garlic	Suet crust pastry using 3–4 oz flour, etc
½ pt white stock	Paprika

Wipe the meat, remove any skin and bone, and cut the meat into pieces. Slice the onions, heat the oil and cook the onions and garlic until light brown. Add the meat and cook quickly until lightly browned. Pour off the surplus fat and add the stock, sauce, seasoning and the bouquet garni. Place in a casserole with a well fitting lid and cook in a moderate oven (180 °C, 350 °F, Gas 4) for 1¼ hr. When ready, remove the bouquet garni and skim off any fat. Have ready 12 small dumplings made from the suet crust pastry. Drop them into the casserole and return to the oven for ½ hr. Serve in the casserole, sprinkled with paprika. Decorate with slices of fresh eating apple.

6 helpings

SAUSAGE CASSEROLE

1 lb pork sausages *or* frankfurters	1 large cooking apple
4 oz onion	1 teasp chopped parsley
1 pt brown sauce	1 teasp dried sage
1 oz margarine	Salt and pepper
2 oz mushrooms	

Fry the sausages gently, turning them, until they are just coloured. Peel and slice the onion, and fry gently in the fat from the sausages. Drain.

Add the margarine to the pan, melt it. Peel, core and slice the apple, and slice the mushrooms. Toss them in the magarine, to fry very lightly.

Transfer all the ingredients to a casserole, sprinkle with the herbs and season well. Heat the oven to 200 °C, 400 °F, Gas Mark 6.

Pour the sauce over the ingredients in the casserole, sprinkle with the herbs and season well. Cook in the oven for 40–50 min, or until the sausages are tender.

4 helpings

CURRIED VEAL OR LAMB

1½ lb lean veal *or* lamb	½ oz grated coconut
2½ oz dripping	1 banana, sliced (optional)
½ lb onions	1 oz raisins (optional)
1 clove garlic, minced (optional)	6 peppercorns
½–1 tablesp curry powder	4 allspice
1 oz ground rice	Cayenne
2 oz chutney	Salt
1 chopped sour apple	2 oz tomato purée
½ oz plum jam	Lemon juice if required
1¼ pt stock	

Trim, wipe and cut meat into 1-in cubes. Melt the dripping in a flame-proof casserole and fry the meat lightly in the hot fat, then remove meat to a plate. Fry the finely sliced onions and garlic until pale golden. Add the curry powder and ground rice and fry all together for about 6 min. Add the chutney, apple, jam, coconut, banana and raisins, if used, spices, seasoning, purée and stock and bring slowly to the boil, stirring constantly. Return meat to the pan. Cover the casserole and place in the oven at 170 °C, 325 °F, Gas Mark 3 for about 1½ hr. Lift the meat on to a hot dish. Add the lemon juice and extra seasoning to the sauce if necessary and strain over the meat. Serve in a border of long grain boiled rice or serve rice separately and a salad of fresh chopped apples with bananas or raisins, tossed in lemon juice.

6 helpings

Poultry and Game Casseroles

GOLDEN HARVEST CHICKEN CASSEROLE

For the marinade:

1 level tablesp clear honey	1 tablesp soy sauce
1 tablesp cider vinegar	4 tablesp dry cider

For the casserole:

1½ oz butter	2 level tablesp plain flour
4 chicken joints	
2 onions, sliced	Scant ½ pt dry cider
1 green bell pepper, seeded and cut in strips	1 15½-oz can peach halves, drained
Salt and pepper	Chopped parsley

Make the marinade first. Put the honey, vinegar, soy sauce and cider into a basin and mix well. Place the chicken joints in a large dish. Pour the marinade over them, and leave for 12 hours, turning once or twice if possible.

When ready to cook, remove chicken from marinade. Melt 1 oz butter in a large frying pan, and brown the chicken quickly on both sides. Remove and drain on kitchen paper. Melt the remaining ½ oz butter in the pan, stir in the flour and cook for 1 min. Remove from the heat, and gradually stir in the mixed marinade and enough cider to make a full ½ pt. Return the mixture to the heat, and bring to the boil, stirring. Season well. Leave aside.

Place the chicken joints, onion and bell pepper in a deep casserole. Pour the cider sauce over them. Cover, and cook at 190°C, 375°F, Gas Mark 5, for 1–1½ hr, depending on the size of the chicken joints. 20 min before the end of the cooking time, add the peach halves to the casserole. Just before serving, sprinkle with chopped parsley.

4 helpings

CHICKEN CREOLE

3½–4 lb chicken *or* fowl, frozen *or* free-range	1 teasp dried thyme
4 oz pickled belly pork	Pinch of salt
1 onion	Pinch of ground black pepper
1 clove of garlic	½ lb okra *or* sweet corn
1 green pepper	
One 14-oz can tomatoes	

Thaw the chicken thoroughly. Cut the pork fat in pieces, and heat. Brown the chicken, then remove it from the pan. Fry the sliced onion, crushed garlic and sliced pepper.

top Chicken in vermouth with walnuts

bottom left Chicken with green peppers

Jugged pigeons ▶

Add the tomatoes, thyme, salt and chicken. Cover and cook slowly. When the chicken is almost tender, stir in the okra in slices, or corn.

Continue cooking until the okra is tender.

6 helpings   *Cooking time 1½–2 hr*

CHICKEN WITH GREEN PEPPERS

4 chicken joints *or* a 2½-lb chicken, cut up	2 tablesp olive oil
1 clove garlic, minced	¼ pt rich chicken stock
3–4 small onions, peeled and quartered	½ gill white wine
	Salt and pepper
3 green bell peppers, seeded and cut in strips	1 tomato, quartered
	1 eating apple, cored and cut in slices

Prepare the chicken joints. Sauté the garlic, onions and peppers in the oil in a flameproof casserole. Remove when tender but not yet brown. Brown the chicken joints in the same fat. Replace the garlic, onions and peppers on the chicken. Add the stock and wine, and season with salt and pepper. Simmer for 40–50 min until the chicken is tender. 10 min before serving, add the tomato and apple.

4 helpings

CHICKEN MARENGO

1 chicken	½ glass sherry (optional)
¼ pt olive oil	
1 pt Espagnole sauce	1 doz button mushrooms
Salt and pepper	6 stoned olives
2 ripe tomatoes	

Garnish:

Fleurons of pastry *or* croûtes of fried bread	Olives
	Mushrooms

Joint the chicken. Remove skin and excess fat. Fry joints in oil until golden brown, drain well, pour away oil. Heat the Espagnole sauce with the tomato pulp, add chicken, sherry (if used), whole olives and mushrooms, and season. Simmer gently until the chicken is tender—about ¾ hr. Pile in the centre of a hot dish, strain sauce over and garnish. Place fleurons or croûtes round the dish.

6 helpings

CHICKEN IN VERMOUTH WITH WALNUTS

1 roasting chicken *or* 4 large chicken joints	½ pt medium dry white vermouth
	Salt and pepper
¾ pt clear chicken stock	Butter
	Flour
1 lb beef bones	10–12 walnut halves
1½ lb soup vegetables (carrots, turnips, celery) cleaned and chopped	

Prepare the chicken by jointing it neatly. Wipe dry. Place the stock, bones and vegetables in the bottom of a deep casserole, and lay a roasting rack or trivel on top. Put the chicken joints on this. Pour the vermouth over the chicken, and sprinkle with salt and pepper.

Cover the casserole tightly, and simmer the contents for 45 min–1¼ hr until the chicken is tender. It will take longer than a 'bake' to cook because it is really being steamed.

When the chicken is ready, strain the sauce. Measure it. Then make a chicken velouté sauce with it, using enough butter and flour for the amount of sauce you have, after straining. Add the walnut halves and simmer for 2–3 minutes while you dish the chicken joints. Pour the sauce over the joints, and decorate the dish with watercress. (Do not serve the soup vegetables.)

4 helpings

POULTRY HOT-POT

1 boiling fowl	½ pt stock *or* water
3 rashers of bacon	½ oz butter
Salt and pepper	½ oz flour
Nutmeg	2 teasp chopped parsley
2 shallots	

Place the giblets from the fowl in the bottom of a casserole. Joint the fowl, remove skin and put joints into casserole, adding bacon (cut in strips), salt, pepper, nutmeg, sliced shallots and the hot stock (or water). Cover tightly, cook in a fairly hot oven (190–200 °C, 375–400 °F, Gas 5–6) for about 2 hr. Knead together butter and flour and add in small pieces to the hot-pot. Add parsley and cook for another ½ hr. Correct seasoning and serve.

This should be served with plain boiled long grain rice.

6 helpings

FULL-COURSE CHICKEN 'BAKE'

1 3-oz can grilling mushrooms	**½ 10-oz pkt frozen peas**
½–¾ pt chicken-noodle soup	**2 tablesp finely-chopped onion**
1 6-oz can evaporated milk	**2 tablesp finely-chopped green bell pepper**
Scant 3 oz butter or margarine	**2 eggs, well beaten**
1¼ oz flour	**¼ teasp salt**
½ teaspoon salt	
Pinch of pepper	
1 lb cooked, boned chicken, diced	

Drain the mushrooms from the can, but keep the liquid. Strain the soup to separate the noodles from it; keep both broth and noodles.

Combine broth, mushroom liquor and milk. Melt the butter, stir in the flour, season with the salt and pepper. Add the broth mixture gradually, and stir over gentle heat until the sauce thickens.

Put the mushrooms, chicken, peas, onions and pepper into a well-greased casserole. Pour the sauce over them. Cover, and bake in the oven at 180 °C, 350 °F, Gas Mark 4 for 25 min. Remove the lid, Top with one of the mixtures in the section on toppings if desired. Bake another 10–20 min, to cook the topping.

DUCK EN CASSEROLE

1 duck	**¾ pt stock (approx.)**
¾ oz flour	
Salt and pepper	**½ pt green peas**
4 oz mushrooms	**1 teasp chopped mint**
4 shallots	

Cut duck into joints, remove all skin, dip the joints in seasoned flour. Place duck, chopped mushrooms and chopped shallots in a casserole. Just cover with stock, put on a tightly-fitting lid and cook in a fairly hot oven (190–200 °C, 375–400 °F, Gas 5–6) about ¾ hr. Add shelled peas and mint and continue cooking until duck is tender—about another ½ hr. Correct seasoning.

Serve from the casserole.

4–5 helpings

BRAISED DUCK WITH CHESTNUTS

1 duck	**1 glass port wine (optional)**
1 pt stock	
Larding bacon (optional)	**1 dessertsp redcurrant jelly**
2 oz butter	
¾ pt Espagnole sauce	

Mirepoix:

2 onions	**Bouquet garni**
1 small turnip	**6 black peppercorns**
2 carrots	
1 stick celery	**2 cloves**

Stuffing:

1 lb chestnuts	**Salt and pepper**
1 large mild onion	**1 egg**

Garnish:

Watercress	**Grapes, apple** *or*
Forcemeat balls	**orange slices**

Boil the chestnuts, remove the skins and chop or mince all but 6 nuts finely for stuffing. Cook the onion in water until tender, chop finely, add to chestnuts, season well and bind with egg. Stuff duck with chestnut mixture, truss, lard with bacon, if liked. Slice the vegetables for the

Chicken Creole

Compote of pigeons

mirepoix foundation, place in a large flame-proof casserole with butter, lay the duck on the vegetables, cover the pan; fry gently for 20 min; then add bouquet garni, spices, and enough stock to cover $\frac{3}{4}$ of the depth of the mirepoix. Cover with a buttered paper, put on lid, simmer gently until duck is tender, for about 2 hr. Add more stock if necessary to prevent burning. Heat the Espagnole sauce, add the 6 nuts, wine (if used) and jelly, re-heat and season to taste. When duck is ready, remove paper and trussing string, and place it in a hot oven (220–230 °C, 425–450 °F, Gas 7–8) to crisp the bacon. Serve on a hot dish, with a watercress or fruit garnish, and forcemeat balls. Serve sauce separately.

4–5 helpings

BRAISED DUCK WITH ORANGE

Cook the duck as in the recipe for Braised Duck with Chestnuts, but use a herb forcemeat stuffing instead of a chestnut one. Add 4 tablesp orange juice to the sauce, and serve it poured over the duck, with a garnish of orange slices or segments.

BRAISED DUCK WITH TURNIPS

1 duck	**Mirepoix of**
1 pt good stock	**vegetables**
3 young turnips	**Glaze**
1 glass sherry	**Salt and pepper**
(optional)	

Cook the duck as in the recipe for Braised Duck with Chestnuts, brush it with warm glaze before crisping in the oven. Mean-while, dice the turnips and boil until tender. Strain the stock; boil it rapidly until it is reduced by half; add sherry, if used, and season to taste.

Serve duck on a hot dish with turnips piled at either end; serve the sauce separately.

4–5 helpings   *Cooking time—about 2 hr*

LARDED AND BRAISED RABBIT

1 rabbit	**Bouquet garni**
Larding bacon	**1 oz butter**
2 oz dripping	**1 oz flour**
Brown stock	
Salt and pepper	

80

Wash, dry, and joint the rabbit; lard each piece with strips of chilled fat bacon. Heat the dripping in a flameproof casserole, fry the rabbit until lightly browned, pour off excess fat, cover with stock, add seasoning and bouquet garni. Cover tightly. Stew gently until rabbit is tender (1¼–1½ hr). Knead butter and flour together and add in small pieces to the stew 20 min before serving. Pile the rabbit on a hot dish; strain the sauce over.

3–4 helpings

COMPOTE OF PIGEONS OR PARTRIDGES

3 pigeons *or* **partridges**	**1 pt good stock**
¼ lb raw ham *or* **bacon**	**Bouquet garni**
	1 carrot
12 shallots *or* **small onions**	**½ turnip**
	1 oz flour
	Salt and pepper
1½ oz butter	**Croûtes of fried bread**

Truss birds for roasting, dice ham or bacon and peel shallots or onions. Melt butter in a flameproof casserole, fry birds, bacon and onions until well browned. Add stock, bring to boiling point; add the bouquet garni, diced carrot and turnip. Cover and allow to simmer steadily until birds are tender, for ¾–1 hr. Remove birds and onions; cut away trussing strings and split birds in half. Keep hot. Blend flour with a little cold water or stock, add to pan. Bring to boiling-point, stirring continuously, re-cover and allow to simmer for 10 min. Season to taste, skim off any excess fat. Serve on a hot dish, pour the sauce over, garnish with the onions and with croûtes of fried bread.

6 helpings

BRAISED GROUSE

Follow the recipe for Compote of Pigeons using a brace of grouse instead of 3 pigeons.

6 helpings   *Cooking time 2 hr, after the braise begins to simmer*

Chicken Marengo in the making

JUGGED PIGEONS

3 pigeons	**Salt and pepper**
3 oz butter	**1 oz flour**
1 onion	**1 glass port** *or*
1 carrot	**claret (optional)**
1 pt good beef stock	

Garnish:

Balls of fried veal forcemeat (optional)

Truss the pigeons as for roasting and fry them until well-browned in 2 oz of the butter. Place the birds in a casserole. Brown the sliced onion and carrot in butter, and add to the pigeons, together with stock and seasoning. Cover and cook in a moderate oven (180 °C, 350 °F, Gas 4) for 1¾ hr. Knead together the flour and remaining 1 oz butter and drop in small pieces into the stock; continue cooking ½ hr, adding wine if used, half-way through this period. Serve pigeons with the sauce poured over, garnished with forcemeat balls if you wish.

6 helpings

PARTY TURKEY—LASAGNE 'BAKE'

8 oz wide lasagne noodles	2 tablesp sliced stuffed green olives
1 15-oz can condensed cream of mushroom soup	2 tablesp finely-chopped onion
Good $\frac{1}{4}$ pt milk	4 tablesp finely-chopped green bell pepper
$\frac{1}{2}$ teasp salt	
$\frac{1}{4}$ teasp ground black pepper	2 tablesp finely-chopped parsley
6 oz cream cheese, softened	1 lb diced cooked turkey
6 oz cottage cheese, sieved	4 oz soft white breadcrumbs, tossed in melted butter

Cook the noodles in boiling, salted water until tender. Rinse under the cold tap. Mix the soup, milk, and seasonings.

Beat the cheeses together, and stir in the olives, onion, green pepper and parsley.

Spread half the noodles in a baking dish about $11\frac{1}{2} \times 7\frac{1}{2} \times 1\frac{1}{2}$ in. Spread with half the cheese mixture, half the turkey, and half the soup mixture. Repeat the layers. Scatter the breadcrumbs on top.

Bake at 190 °C, 375 °F, Gas Mark 5 for 30 min or until well heated and bubbling. Let stand for 10 min before serving.

8 helpings

RABBIT STEW—RICH

1 rabbit	1 pt good stock
4 oz streaky bacon	Bouquet garni
18 button onions	2 cloves
2 oz butter	Salt and pepper
$1\frac{1}{2}$ oz flour	1 glass claret (optional)

Wash, dry and joint the rabbit, put the liver aside. Dice the bacon, peel the onions. Melt the butter in a large flameproof casserole, fry onions and bacon until brown, then lift out. Fry rabbit lightly, sprinkle in flour and continue frying until well browned. Replace the onions and bacon, add hot stock, bouquet garni, cloves and seasoning, cover tightly and stew gently until rabbit is tender (about $1\frac{1}{4}$ hr). About 15 min before serving, add the claret if used, put in the liver (washed and cut into small pieces) and finish cooking. Pile the rabbit on a hot dish, strain the sauce over and garnish with the bacon dice and onions.

3–4 helpings   *Cooking time about 2 hr*

JUGGED HARE

1 hare	12 peppercorns
3 oz butter	Bouquet garni
Salt and pepper	$1\frac{1}{2}$ pt stock
1 onion	1 oz flour
4 cloves	Veal forcemeat
1 glass port *or* claret (optional)	Fat for frying
1 tablesp lemon juice	Redcurrant jelly

Prepare the hare and cut into neat small pieces. Heat 2 oz. of the butter, and fry the pieces of hare in it until brown. Put the hare in a casserole with salt, onion stuck with cloves, half the wine (if used), lemon juice, peppercorns, bouquet garni and hot stock. Place a tight lid on the casserole, book in a moderate oven (180 °C, 350 °F, Gas 4) about 3 hr. Knead the flour and remaining butter together, stir into the stock about $\frac{1}{2}$ hr before serving. Add the remaining wine too, and season to taste. Form forcemeat into small balls and fry. Gently heat the blood from hare, stir into the gravy, allow to thicken. Serve hare piled on a hot dish, strain sauce over, and arrange the forcemeat balls round dish. Serve with redcurrant jelly handed separately.

5–6 helpings

Seafood, Egg and Cheese Casseroles and 'Bakes'

CREAMED COD AND APPLE IN POTATO RING

2 tablesp finely-chopped onion	1 tablesp butter
2½ oz butter or margarine	Pinch of nutmeg
1½ oz flour	2 egg yolks, slightly beaten
½ pt fish or vegetable stock	1¼ lb cooked cod or haddock
½ gill white wine	4 oz fresh apple, peeled, cored and diced, dipped in lemon juice
½ pt single cream	
2 teasp salt	
1 large pkt instant mashed potato	1 6-oz can grilling mushrooms, drained
Salt and freshly-ground black pepper	

In a fireproof casserole, sauté the onion in the butter or margarine until tender but not brown. Stir in the flour. Add the stock and wine gradually, stirring to blend, over gentle heat. When the mixture thickens, add the cream and remove from the heat.

Make up the potato with the seasoning, butter and nutmeg as directed. Pack into a greased ring mould.

Stir a little of the sauce into the egg yolks. Return this mixture to the rest of the sauce. Add the fish, cut in fairly large pieces, and the apple. Add the mushrooms. Heat gently for 2–3 min without boiling, to thicken the sauce.

Turn out the mashed potato on to a serving plate, and place under a moderate grill flame for 2–3 min, to brown. Fill the centre of the ring with the fish and apple mixture. Decorate with chopped watercress before serving, if desired.

6–8 helpings

CASSEROLED SEAFOOD SUPPER 'BAKE'

1 lb white fish fillets (cod or haddock)	4 tomatoes, sliced
1 pt milk	1 large pkt instant mashed potato
2 oz butter	2 oz peeled, cooked shrimps or prawns
Salt and pepper	
2 oz flour	
4 eggs	
6 rashers thin bacon, without rinds	

Skin the fish fillets, and cut in pieces. Warm the milk. Put the fish, ½ oz butter, salt and pepper and ½ pt of the milk in a casserole. Cook in the oven for 20 min at 170 °C, 325 °F, Gas Mark 3, covered.

Melt the remaining butter in a saucepan, add the flour and cook together gently for

Creamed cod in potato ring

2–3 min without browning. Gradually add the rest of the milk, and stir until the sauce thickens. Add the liquid from the fish casserole, and stir it in. Hard-boil 2 eggs and beat the other 2 in a basin until liquid. Chop the hard-boiled eggs and add to the fish, with the sauce. Grill the bacon lightly, and place the rashers neatly on the fish, egg and sauce mixture, then top with the sliced tomatoes. Sprinkle with salt and pepper.

Make up the mashed potato as directed, and add one of the beaten eggs. Spread it gently with a fork all over the tomatoes. Brush with the rest of the egg. Bake for 20–30 min at 180 °C, 350 °F, Gas Mark 4. Just before the end of the cooking time, decorate with the shrimps or prawns and let them heat through briefly.

HERRINGS TAILS-IN-AIR

4 herrings	**1 green pepper,**
2 oz fresh	**seeded and**
breadcrumbs	**sliced**
1 small onion,	**A little milk if**
grated	**needed**
1 level tablesp	**Salt and pepper**
chopped	**to taste**
parsley	**$\frac{1}{4}$–$\frac{1}{2}$ pt tomato**
1 small tomato,	**soup, fresh** *or*
chopped	**canned**
1 onion, sliced	

Scale the herrings and remove the heads, then clean and bone them but leave the tails on. Keep the roes. Trim the tails and cut off the fins with kitchen scissors. Chop the roes and mix with the crumbs, grated onion, chopped parsley and tomato;

84

Casserole of shellfish with rice

season and bind with milk if needed. Lay the herrings flat on a board, put 1 tablesp stuffing on the head end of each and roll up towards the tail. Place tightly in a deep fireproof casserole, and scatter over the sliced onion and green pepper. Pour the soup over. Cover the casserole, and bake in a fairly hot oven (200°C, 400°F, Gas 6) for 30 min.

AUBERGINES WITH POACHED EGGS

3 aubergines	Salt and pepper
½ oz butter	6 small poached
¼ pt tomato pulp	eggs
2 tablesp chopped ham	Chopped parsley
1 tablesp breadcrumbs	

Boil the aubergines in slightly salted water until tender, or steam them. Halve them lengthwise, and remove seeds if necessary. Heat the butter, add the tomato pulp, ham, breadcrumbs and stir over heat. Season well, then fill the cavities of the aubergines with the mixture. Put into a greased dish in a moderate oven (180°C, 350°F, Gas 4) and heat thoroughly. Place a neatly trimmed poached egg on each half; garnish with parsley and serve.

6 helpings   Cooking time about 1 hr altogether

SUZY WONG CASSEROLE

1 lb peeled prawns	1 tablesp cooking oil
8-oz can soya beans	2 tablesp finely-chopped onion
¼ teasp Tabasco sauce	1 teasp curry powder
Juice of ½ lemon	¼ pt white wine
8-oz can bamboo shoots	½ pt fish velouté sauce (see recipe)
8-oz can pineapple rings	¼ pt double cream

Marinate the prawns and soya beans with the Tabasco sauce and lemon juice for about 2 hr. Cut the bamboo shoots and pineapple rings into thick strips. Heat the oil in a flameproof casserole, and sauté the onion until golden-brown. Sprinkle with the curry powder and stir well. Add the wine. Leave until 10 min before serving time.

Reduce the wine by about half over fairly rapid heat. Add all the remaining ingredients. Cook for 5 min, and season to taste.

Serve topped with chopped parsley and whole prawns if you wish.

NOTE: Make the fish velouté sauce exactly like a white sauce but use fish stock instead of milk.

4–6 helpings

CASSEROLE OF SHELLFISH WITH RICE

2 tablesp finely-chopped onion	6 oz uncooked rice
2 tablesp butter *or* margarine	2 8-oz cups firmly packed with cooked shell-fish (lobster and crab meat, sliced scallops, prawns)
2 tablesp flour	
½ teasp salt	
Pinch of pepper	
1½ gills single cream	
½ teasp Worcester sauce	5 oz cooked rice
1 3-oz can grilling mushrooms, drained and sliced	1 green bell pepper, seeded and sliced
	12 unshelled cooked prawns

Sauté the onion in the butter until tender but not brown. Blend in the flour and seasoning. Gradually stir in the cream and Worcester sauce and stir over very gentle heat until the sauce is thick. Stir in the sliced mushrooms and leave aside.

In a saucepan, boil the uncooked rice to serve with the casserole dish.

Place the shellfish and cooked rice in a greased shallow casserole, and add the mushroom and onion sauce. Heat almost (but not quite) to boiling point. Add the sliced pepper and simmer for 2–3 min.

Serve the casserole dish with the plain rice heaped round the shellfish mixture. Decorate with the unshelled prawns.

4 helpings

POTATO AND BACON CASSEROLE

6 large raw potatoes, peeled and coarsely grated	2 eggs
	1 teasp grated onion
	1 tablesp flour
4–5 bacon rashers, cooked and crumbled	Salt and freshly-ground black pepper
	Sour cream
3 tablesp bacon fat	

Mix all the ingredients except the sour cream. Place in a shallow casserole rubbed with bacon fat. Bake at 180 °C, 350 °F, Gas Mark 4, for 40 min or until potatoes are soft. Serve with the sour cream in a jug.

4 helpings

STUFFED CABBAGE

6 large leaves of cabbage	Powdered mace
	Pepper and salt
4 oz cooked rice	Worcester sauce
2 teasp very finely chopped onion	Stock
	4 oz fresh minced meat
2 chopped hard-boiled eggs	Arrowroot

Wash and boil the cabbage leaves for 5 min in salt water. Drain. Mix the filling, moistening it with stock and flavouring it carefully. Form into rolls. Remove a little of the coarse vein of the cabbage leaves. Wrap each roll of filling in a cabbage leaf and tie with cotton or secure with a cocktail stick. Place in a shallow casserole, barely cover with stock, put on lid and simmer very gently 45 min. Lift on to a hot dish and thicken stock by boiling it with blended arrowroot (1 teasp to ¼ pt of stock). Season carefully. Pour sauce over cabbage rolls and serve immediately.

6 helpings

TOMATO PILAF WITH EGGS

2 oz butter	2 fresh tomatoes,
7 oz uncooked	skinned and
rice	chopped
½ pt beef stock or	3 tablesp chopped
bouillon	parsley
Generous ¼ pt	Salt and pepper
tomato juice	Poached eggs

Melt the butter in a flameproof casserole. Add the rice. Stir until the grains are coated and yellow. Heat and add the stock and tomato juice together. Add the tomatoes, and sprinkle parsley, salt and pepper on top. Cover and bake at 180 °C, 350 °F, Gas Mark 4, for 30–40 min or until liquid is absorbed. Top with poached eggs just before serving.

4 helpings

BEAN AND TOMATO CASSEROLE

4 spring onions,	½ teasp sugar
cleaned and	Salt
chopped	Pinch of cayenne
3 tablesp olive oil	pepper
1 lb dried haricot	1 30-oz can
beans soaked	tomatoes
overnight and	Parmesan cheese
simmered	
until tender	
½ green bell	
pepper, seeded	
and chopped	

Sauté the onions gently in the oil until tender. Add the beans and green pepper. Toss in the fat, then transfer to a greased casserole. Sprinkle with seasonings. Cover with the tomatoes, and sprinkle generously

with cheese. Bake, uncovered for 40 min at 180 °C, 350 °F, Gas Mark 4.

8 helpings

CELERY AND CHEESE CASSEROLE

2 bunches celery,	Salt and pepper
cleaned and	½ pt milk
cut in 1-in	1 tablesp chopped
pieces (inner	green pepper
sticks only)	without seeds
1 tablesp butter	1 lb fresh garden
1 tablesp flour	peas
½ teasp dried	3 tablesp grated
sweet basil	cheese

Parboil the celery sticks for 15 min. Meanwhile make a creamy white sauce with the butter, flour, seasonings and milk. Stir in all the vegetables. Turn into a shallow buttered casserole, and sprinkle with cheese. Bake at 200 °C, 400 °F, Gas Mark 6, for 15–20 min.

4 helpings

More Good 'Bakes'

ONE-DISH 'BAKES' with vegetables and a padding such as *pasta* in them are one of the best American gifts to Western cookery. In the close-packed activities of modern life, they are invaluable, especially for housewives who work during the days. It is hard to know what we would do without them, since they are easy to prepare and serve, and make little washing-up. Many of them, too, have the added convenience of being made with 'instant' and ready-packed foods which you can keep in the store-cupboard without risk of spoiling, for whenever they are needed.

With a little care, too, you can choose a pudding which will oven-cook in the same time as the main 'bake', and so make your whole meal by one process, simply by turning on the oven. You can even reheat a sauce in its jug on the oven floor at the same time, by standing it in a tray of hot water, and making sure the top is sealed with foil.

HAMBURGER AND POTATO FLUFF PIE

1 medium-sized onion, peeled and chopped	10½-oz can condensed Tomato soup
1 tablesp clean dripping	5 medium-sized potatoes, cooked, peeled and still hot
1 lb minced beef	
¾ teasp salt	
Pinch of pepper	¼ pt milk
½ lb green beans, frozen or fresh, thawed, drained and sliced	1 small egg, beaten

Fry the onion gently in the heated dripping until soft but not brown. Add the beef, salt and pepper. Brown lightly on all sides. Pour into a shallow casserole, and stir so that the fat seeps through the solid ingredients and coats the base and sides of the dish.

Lay the beans on top, in a flat layer. Spread the soup over them.

Mash the hot potatoes. Mix in the milk and egg lightly with a fork. Season, and place in mounds on top of the casserole. (Use 'instant' mashed potato if you prefer.) Bake at 180 °C, 350 °F, Gas 4, for 25–30 min.

6 helpings

BAKED BEEF CAKE

1 lb cold roast beef	4 oz bread-crumbs
2 oz bread raspings (brown or toasted crumbs)	1 teasp chopped parsley
	Salt and pepper
	1 egg
	1 gill stock
2 oz cooked ham *or* bacon	Gravy *or* brown sauce
1 oz butter *or* fat	Parsley sprigs
1 small onion	

Grease a plain mould or shallow cake-tin and put in the bread raspings. Shake the mould until it is well covered with raspings. Mince the beef and bacon or ham finely. Melt the fat and fry the finely-chopped onion until slightly brown and add to the minced meats. Then mix together with the bread-crumbs, chopped parsley, seasoning, egg and stock. Use more stock if the mixture is very dry. Place the mixture in the prepared mould, pressing down well. Cover with greased paper and bake in a fairly hot oven at 190 °C, 375 °F, Gas 5 for about 45 min. Turn out carefully on to a hot dish and pour a little sauce or gravy around. Garnish with parsley sprigs.

6 helpings

AMERICAN SALAMAGUNDI

5 oz uncooked rice	1 lb minced beef
1 teasp salt	12 oz frozen sweet corn, thawed, drained
Pinch of pepper	
¾ pt Condensed Tomato soup	
¼ pt hot water	1 teasp chilli powder
⅛ pt stock or bouillon	4 rashers smoked bacon without rind
1 oz dried onion flakes, soaked	
½ green bell pepper, blanched and chopped (seeds removed)	

Place the rice in a layer in an ungreased casserole. Sprinkle with salt and pepper. Pour over ½ the soup, water and stock mixed. Scatter over the onion flakes and chopped bell pepper, fork over the mince to break up any lumps, then add to the casserole.

Sprinkle with salt and top with the corn. Smooth the mixture flat.

Add the chilli powder to the remaining soup; mix in the rest of the water and stock.

Pour the soup over the corn, lay on the bacon rashers, cover the casserole, and bake for 1 hr at 180 °C, 350 °F, Gas 4. Uncover, and bake 15 min longer, or till rice is tender when you plunge a fork through the mixture.

A cold curry sauce or dip goes well with this spicy dish.

5–6 helpings

SPICED TOPSIDE BAKE

2 lb topside cut in 1-in thick slices	3 large potatoes, peeled and halved
2 teasp salt	1 bay leaf
¼ teasp pepper	1 10½-oz can
Flour to dredge	Condensed
6 medium-sized onions, peeled and sliced	Tomato soup
	½ lb frozen, sliced green beans, thawed
2 oz cooking fat or clean dripping	1 slice French bread per person

Season the meat well, and dredge thoroughly with the flour on both sides. Sauté the onions in the fat until soft but not brown. Remove, and sauté the meat in the same fat gently, until brown on both sides. Place in a large, deep ovenproof casserole. Add the onions, potatoes and bay leaf. Top with the soup as it comes from the can, and cover the dish closely with foil and a lid. Bake at 180 °C, 350 °F, Gas 4 for 1¾hr or until the meat is tender. Add the beans, drained, and bake for a further 15 min. Toast the French bread slices. Arrange them round the edge of a serving plate, pile the meat and vegetables in the centre, and serve very hot.

6–8 helpings

ECONOMY ONE-DISH STEAK MEAL

1½ lb chuck beef cut in 1-in slices	2 sticks celery cut in 1-in pieces
1 pkt dehydrated white onion soup	3 small potatoes, peeled and halved
2 medium-sized carrots, cleaned and quartered	2 tablesp margarine
	½ teasp salt

Cut a sheet of foil 2½ ft × 18 in. Sprinkle dry onion soup over each slice of meat and pile the slices in the centre of the foil. Cover with the vegetables. Flake the margarine and scatter the flakes on the vegetables. Sprinkle with salt.

Wrap the foil securely round the food to seal in any juices. Place the parcel on a baking sheet, and bake at high heat, at 220 °C, 425 °F, Gas 7, for about 1½ hr or until the meat is tender. Place the parcel on a heated serving dish, and unwrap at the table to let the first aroma strike everyone present.

4 helpings

SIMPLE BAKED SAVOURY PUDDING

8 oz stale bread	1 egg
¼–½ pint milk or milk and water	1 or 2 kinds of fresh herbs, such as parsley and sage
½ medium onion, peeled and chopped small	Salt and pepper
1 heaped tablesp oatmeal	1 heaped tablesp flour

Soak the bread in the milk until it is soft. Mash it well with a fork. Add the onion, oatmeal and flour, and then the flavouring herbs. Beat the egg, and mix in thoroughly. Season to suit your taste, fairly strongly. Spread the dough in a small greased baking tin to a depth of about an inch. Bake at 200 °C, 400 °F, Gas 6 for 7–10 minutes, then lower heat to 180 °C, 350 °F, Gas 4 and bake a further 30 minutes or until crisp and brown.

LAMB CHARLOTTE, BAKED

1¼ lb cold cooked mutton	3 shallots
	Salt and pepper
2 tablesp browned breadcrumbs	2 eggs
8 tablesp white breadcrumbs	2 tablesp mushroom ketchup
3 teasp finely-chopped parsley	A little gravy (leftover)
	6 small tomatoes
	1 oz butter

Dice or mince the lamb. Well grease a plain mould or cake-tin and cover with browned breadcrumbs. Mix together the meat, white breadcrumbs, parsley, the finely-chopped shallots and the salt, pepper, beaten eggs, mushroom ketchup and just enough gravy to moisten slightly. Put the mixture into the prepared tin and bake gently in a cool oven at 150 °C, 300 °F, Gas 2 for 1½ hr until firm and set. 20 min before the end of the cooking time, place the warmed tomatoes in a shallow baking tray, dot with the butter and bake on the top oven shelf, above the charlotte, while it finishes cooking. When it is cooked, unmould the charlotte carefully on to a hot dish. Garnish with the baked tomatoes and serve with the gravy oven-heated in an ovenproof jug below the charlotte for the past 10 min.

6 helpings

LAMB AND YOGURT MOUSSAKA BAKE

2 tablesp cooking oil	¾ lb potatoes, parboiled, peeled and thinly sliced
1 large onion, peeled, blanched and chopped	2 aubergines
1 lb cooked minced lamb	1 lb tomatoes, skinned and sliced

For the sauce:

1 oz butter	½ teasp garlic powder
1 oz flour	½ teasp salt
½ pt milk	Pinch of white pepper
2 oz grated mild cheese	

For the topping:

1 egg	Salt and pepper
1 oz flour	Paprika
¼ pt natural yogurt	

Heat the oil in a frying pan. Sauté the onion gently until soft. Add the lamb and fry for 5 min, turning over with a spoon to brown it. Leave aside.

Melt the butter for the sauce in a saucepan. Stir in the flour gradually and cook for 2–3 min without browning. Remove from heat, and stir in the milk, also gradually, stirring to blend without lumps. Bring gently to the boil, and cook until the sauce thickens slightly. Remove from the heat and stir in the cheese, then season as it suits you.

Put ½ the potato slices in the bottom of a deep casserole of 8 in diameter, in a neat layer. Top with ½ of each of the other main ingredients, onion, lamb, aubergines (skinned and sliced) tomatoes.

Cover this layer with a layer of the cheese sauce. Season. Repeat the layers, ending with a potato layer. Bake at 190 °C, 375 °F, Gas 5 for about 1 hr.

Blend the egg and flour to a smooth paste. Stir in the yogurt. Pour the mixture over the bake, and continue baking for about 20 min, until the topping is bubbling and browning.

4–6 helpings

PORK FILLETS IN ROQUEFORT SAUCE

6 oz flat egg noodles	¾ teasp rock or sea salt
6 good slices pork fillet, ½-in thick	Pinch ground black pepper
1¼ tablesp white cooking fat or lard	1½ gills milk
½ teasp salt	8 oz crumbled Roquefort cheese
Pinch of white pepper	3 tablesp green bell pepper, blanched and chopped
3 tablesp margarine	
3 tablesp plain flour	3 tablesp pimento, chopped

Cook the noodles in boiling, salted water until *al dente*. Drain. Brown the meat gently in the fat, taking 10–15 min to brown both sides. Season.

Melt the margarine gently in a small saucepan. Blend in the flour, rock or sea salt, and pepper. Gradually trickle in the milk, stirring. Continue cooking, still stirring until the sauce thickens. Add the cheese, and stir until it melts and the sauce thickens again.

Mix together the noodles, green bell pepper, pimento and blue-cheese mixture. Spread in an ungreased baking tin or shallow casserole about 10 × 6 × 1½ in. in size. Lay the meat on top. Bake at 180 °C, 350 °F, Gas 4, for 30–40 min. Serve from the dish.

6 helpings

MOULDED LAMB BAKE

¾ lb cooked lamb	1 teasp
Browned bread-	finely-chopped
crumbs	parsley
½ oz butter	½ teasp
1 shallot *or* onion,	powdered
finely chopped	mixed herbs
⅓ pt stock *or* milk	1 egg
½ lb mashed	Salt and pepper
potatoes	½ pt brown sauce
2 tablesp white	
breadcrumbs	

Chop the meat finely. Grease a plain mould or basin and coat it thickly with browned breadcrumbs. Melt the butter in a saucepan. Fry the finely-chopped onion until well browned. Then add the stock, and when boiling put in the potatoes, meat, white breadcrumbs, parsley, herbs, egg and a good seasoning of salt and pepper. Stir over heat until thoroughly hot, then turn into the prepared mould. Bake in a moderate oven at 180 °C, 350 °F, Gas 4 for 30–40 min, or until the mixture is firm enough to be turned out of the mould. Heat the sauce in an ovenproof jug on the oven floor. Serve the moulded bake hot with the gravy poured round it.

5–6 helpings

BAKED STUFFED BREAST OF LAMB

1 breast lamb	1 oz lamb fat or
	dripping
For the filling:	2 teasp
2 oz white	granulated
breadcrumbs	sugar
1 oz currants	1 egg yolk
2 dates, stoned	2 teasp single
and chopped	cream or top
¼ teasp each	of the milk
ground mace	
and cloves	

Lay the breast of lamb out flat. Make a 'pudding' or stiff stuffing of the other ingredients: first mix all the dry ingredients and the fat; then mix together the egg yolk, and the cream. Spread this mixture over the lamb, and roll up like a Swiss roll. Tie the roll with string, or skewer it firmly.

Place in a small baking-tin on a rack, and cover it (if lean) with a little fat or dripping. Bake at 220 °C, 425 °F, Gas 7 for 10 minutes, then lower the heat to 180 °C, 350 °F, Gas 4 for a further 30–35 minutes. Remove the thread or skewer, and keep warm on a dish, while you make pan-gravy with 1 tablesp of fat from the baking-tin, 1 tablesp flour, and ¼ pint stock. A few drops of claret and a little nutmeg improve the gravy.

Bake and serve this Baked Savoury Pudding with the lamb.

YOGURT-MARINATED LAMB CUTLETS

8 lamb cutlets	½ teasp garlic
	powder
For the	
marinade:	For the
1 pt natural	additional
yogurt	"padding":
1 teasp curry	8 oz Patna rice
powder	¼ teasp saffron
1 teasp mixed	strands
herbs	
½ teasp turmeric	For garnish:
or saffron	Parsley sprigs
strands	Cooked peas

Place the cutlets in a shallow casserole. Spike with a fork. Mix together the yogurt, curry powder, herbs, turmeric or saffron strands (soaked for 10 min in boiling water) and the garlic powder. Pour this mixture over the lamb, and leave to marinate for 24 hr. When ready to cook, baste the lamb with the marinade. Bake the dish in the marinade at 190 °C, 375 °F. Gas 5, for 55–60 min, without a lid.

About 25 min before the end of the cooking time, when the marinade is nearly absorbed, cook the rice in boiling salted water, to which the extra saffron strands are added. Drain after 10 min while the rice (now slightly yellowed) is still *al dente*. Place on an ovenproof serving dish, cover with a damp cloth, and place on top of the lamb to steam for a few minutes. Place the peas in a container on the oven floor.

To serve, remove from the oven, place the cutlets and any remaining marinade on top

Dumplings make this casserole really satisfying

of the rice, and garnish with the parsley sprigs and peas.

4 helpings

BAKED PORK AND APPLES

2 tablesp cooking oil	4 small apples, cored but not peeled, cut in quarters
3 medium-sized onions, blanched and peeled	1 lb canned new potatoes, drained and sliced
4 slices cooked leg of pork, 1-in thick	$\frac{1}{4}$ pt white stock or bouillon
1 teasp salt	
Pinch of pepper	

This one-dish family dinner needs minimal cooking. Heat the oil in a frying pan. Slice the onions, and sauté them until soft but not brown. Drain on soft kitchen paper, and brown the pork slices lightly in the same fat. Season them with the salt and pepper, and remove to the soft paper to drain.

Swill the remaining fat all over the inside of a shallow ovenproof bake-and-serve dish, to coat it. Lay the pork slices in the dish, overlapping slightly. Arrange the onion and the apple quarters all over them. Top with the sliced potatoes laid in neat rows. Season again.

Add $\frac{1}{8}$-$\frac{1}{4}$ pt stock or bouillon to the frying pan, stir to include the crusty bits and pan juices in it, and pour over the meat and

93

vegetables. Cover the dish tightly with foil, and bake at 180 °C, 350 °F, Gas 4 for 40–50 min. Uncover and bake 5–10 min more, to brown the top.

Serve with green salad.

4 helpings

PORK RIBS WITH SPICED SAUERKRAUT

3 lb breast ribs of pork (American spareribs)	1 cooking apple cored but not peeled, chopped
2 teasp salt	$\frac{1}{2}$ pt tomato juice
$\frac{1}{4}$ teasp pepper	2 tablesp
Sauerkraut as side dish for 6 people	Demerara sugar
2 medium-sized carrots, cleaned and shredded	3 teasp caraway seeds

Cut the ribs into serving portions, and roll them in seasoning. Mix the sauerkraut, its liquid (if canned) and all the remaining ingredients. Place the mixture in a deep, greased, overproof casserole. Put the ribs on top, seal the casserole closely with foil and then a lid and bake at 180 °C, 350 °F, Gas 4 for $\frac{1}{2}$ hr. Unwrap the foil and spoon the sauerkraut mixture over the ribs. Re-cover, and bake at the same temperature for 2–3 hr, or until the ribs are really tender. During the last hr, baste the ribs again, 3 or 4 times.

Serve straight from the casserole, making sure that each helping has sauce from the sauerkraut with it. Much of the dish's health value is in the sauce.

4–6 helpings

BATTER PUDDING WITH GAME

Batter as for Savoury Batter Pudding

About $\frac{3}{4}$ lb cooked game meat (leftover roast game is suitable)	$\frac{1}{2}$ oz. butter Brown or Piquant Sauce

Prepare the batter as for the Savoury Sausage Batter Pudding, cover and leave to stand for 30 min. Sprinkle the meat with seasoning, dice it, removing any gristle or bones. Spread the meat in a layer over the bottom of a Yorkshire Pudding tin, flake the butter over it, and heat in the oven at 220 °C, 425 °F, Gas 7 until the butter sizzles and just begins to smoke. Pour the batter over the meat and cook like the Savoury Sausage Batter Pudding. 10–15 min before the end of the cooking time, put the sauce in a jug or gravy boat on the floor of the oven, covered with a plate, to heat through.

6 helpings

SAVOURY SAUSAGE BATTER PUDDING, BAKED

1 lb plain flour	1 tablesp cooking fat or lard
$\frac{1}{4}$ teasp each salt and pepper	Grated cheese
2 eggs	About $\frac{3}{4}$ lb sausage meat
1 pt milk	

Make the batter. Sift the flour, salt and pepper together. Make a well in the centre of the flour, and break the eggs into it. Add about $\frac{1}{4}$ pt milk. Stir, working the flour down into the mixture, and adding more milk as you need it to make a stiff batter. Beat well, and leave to stand, while you grate the cheese and prepare the sausage meat.

Put a little of the fat into a Yorkshire pudding tin, mix in the sausage meat and fry gently (or bake-fry at high heat on the top shelf of the oven, or grill) until the meat begins to sizzle and brown, turning over with a spoon to cook both sides. Remove tin from heat, add the rest of the fat and spread the meat in a flat layer over it. Heat in the oven at 220 °C, 425 °F, Gas 7 until the fat just begins to smoke. Quickly pour in the batter, and leave to bake until the batter rises and begins to brown. Reduce the heat to 190 °C, 375 °F, Gas 5 and finish cooking for 10–15 min more. Serve with the cheese sprinkled over the dish.

Chutney makes a good side dish for this pudding, and so do segments of chilled tomato.

6 helpings

HAM AND ASPARAGUS BAKE

6-oz can evaporated milk	3 tablesp dried onion flakes, soaked overnight
2 tablesp water	
12–14 oz cooked ham in the piece, in $\frac{1}{2}$-in cubes	8–10 oz frozen asparagus spears
10–12 oz cooked rice	1 oz cornflake crumbs
3 oz mild cheesed, shredded	3 tablesp melted butter
10$\frac{1}{2}$-oz can condensed Cream of Mushroom soup	

Pour the evaporated milk into a basin, add the water, and then the ham, rice, cheese, soup (not thinned) and onion. Stir thoroughly to blend, and to coat the solid ingredients. Pour boiling water over the asparagus spears to separate them, then drain them.

Place half the main mixture in a shallow bake-and-serve dish. Cover with a layer of asparagus, then top with the remaining mixture.

Top the cornflake crumbs with the butter, and coat well. Sprinkle all over the meat dish. Bake at 180 °C, 350 °F, Gas 4 for 20–25 min or until top is lightly browned and mixture is bubbling beneath.

4–6 helpings

HAM AND EGG SUPPER

About 1 lb canned ham, cubed	$\frac{1}{8}$ (scant) rich milk
6 hard-boiled eggs, sliced	4 oz coarsely-grated Cheddar cheese
6 oz canned grilling mushrooms, drained	3–4 drops Tabasco Sauce
10$\frac{1}{2}$-oz can Condensed Cream of Celery soup	About 5 oz soft white breadcrumbs

Place alternate layers of ham, egg and mushrooms in a deep ovenproof casserole, beginning and ending with ham. Mix the soup with nearly all the milk in a saucepan, then stir in the cheese and Tabasco and mix well. Heat gently, just till the cheese melts, then pour over the casseroled mixture. Spread the breadcrumbs all over. Sprinkle with the remaining milk. Bake uncovered at 190 °C, 375 °F, Gas 5 for 20–25 min until heated through and the crumbs are golden.

6 helpings

VEAL AND HAM BAKED CAKE

$\frac{3}{4}$ lb cold cooked veal *or* veal and ham mixed	1 teasp grated lemon rind
2 tablesp raspings (browned or toasted breadcrumbs)	Pinch of nutmeg
	1 large egg
	2–3 tablesp gravy *or* milk
1 small onion	Salt and pepper
3 oz white breadcrumbs	Gravy, tomato *or* brown sauce
1$\frac{1}{2}$ teasp finely-chopped parsley	Parsley

Grease a plain round mould or cake-tin and coat it well with raspings. Remove all skin and gristle, and chop or mince the meat finely. Add to the meat the finely-chopped onion, the breadcrumbs, parsley, lemon rind, nutmeg, beaten egg and as much gravy or milk as is required to moisten well. Season highly. Press the mixture into the prepared tin and cover with greased paper. Bake in a fairly hot oven at 200 °C, 400 °F, Gas 6 for about 40 min. Turn out the cake on to a hot dish. Pour some of the gravy or sauce round and serve the rest separately. Garnish with parsley.

4 helpings

Sweet Casseroles and 'Bakes'

A GREAT MANY puddings and desserts benefit in food value and flavour from the long, slow cooking which casseroles make possible. They are first-class value for the budget-wise housewife too.

APRICOT AND NUT CASSEROLE

1 lb dried apricots	3 tablesp butter, melted
Water to cover	4 oz wholemeal
Sugar to suit your taste	brown breadcrumbs
3 dessertsp soft brown sugar	1½–2 oz chopped walnuts

Mix the apricots, water and sugar in a casserole. Leave in the oven overnight, covered, at the lowest possible heat. Next day, drain. Keep the juice.

Mix the brown sugar, butter, breadcrumbs and walnuts. Replace 1 layer of apricots in the casserole, and spread lightly with the crumb mixture. Repeat the layers until all the ingredients are used ending with a crumb topping. Trickle in the juice from the apricots until it covers about 2/3rds of the pudding. Bake at 180 °C, 350 °F Gas Mark 4, uncovered, for 40–50 min.

4 helpings

CARAMEL RICE PUDDING

3 oz loaf sugar	2 eggs
½ gill water	1½ oz castor sugar
4½ oz rice	Pinch of salt
2 pt milk	

Heat a heavy flameproof casserole, and have ready a thick oven-cloth to hold it with. Heat the loaf sugar and water in the casserole without stirring. When it turns light brown, lift the casserole quickly from the heat and rotate to coat the inside of the casserole. It can burn very quickly.

Put the caramel-lined casserole in a cold place, say on a stone floor. When it is cool, scatter in the rice, add the milk. Whisk the eggs until liquid with the sugar and salt, and mix in. Cover the casserole tightly, stand it in a baking tray of hot water and bake it at not more than 140 °C, 275 °F, Gas Mark ½ overnight. Unmould while still hot, leave to cool and serve cold with cream.

Caramel rice pudding

BROWN BETTY PUDDING

6 oz breadcrumbs	**4 oz demerara**
2 lb cooking	**sugar**
apples	**2 tablesp water**
1 lemon	
4 tablesp golden	
syrup	

Grease a 2 pt casserole. Coat it with a layer of breadcrumbs. Peel, core and thinly slice the apples. Fill the pie-dish with alternate layers of apples, grated lemon rind and breadcrumbs. Heat the syrup, sugar and water in a pan, add the lemon juice and pour this over the mixture. Bake at 170 °C, 325 °F, Gas Mark 3 for 1¼–1½ hr until the pudding is brown and the apple cooked.

6 helpings

CHESTNUT PUDDING

6 oz chestnuts,	**2 oz butter** *or*
weighed after	**margarine**
the skins have	**2 oz flour**
been removed	**2 oz cake crumbs**
Pinch of salt	**3 eggs**
1 oz plain	**½ teasp vanilla**
chocolate	**essence**
½ pt milk	**1 oz castor sugar**

Wash the chestnuts, make a slit in each and boil in water for about 10 min. Remove both skins and put the chestnuts into a saucepan with a very little water and the salt. Cook until tender, strain, dry and rub through a fine sieve.

Grate the chocolate and put it in the milk and simmer until dissolved. Allow to cool slightly.

97

In another pan melt the fat, stir in the flour, cook for 2–3 min. Work in the milk and chocolate gradually, keeping the mixture smooth: stir until it boils. Add the cake crumbs and continue cooking until the mixture leaves the sides of the pan. Allow to cool. Separate the eggs. Beat into the mixture the egg yolks, chestnut purée, vanilla essence and sugar. Whisk the egg whites to a stiff froth and fold them lightly into the mixture. Pour into a well-buttered casserole. Cover with buttered paper and a lid. Bake in a fairly hot oven (190 °C, 375 °F, Gas 5) for 1 hr.

Serve with vanilla or custard sauce.

6–7 helpings

CHOCOLATE AND BRANDY CREAM

8 oz plain chocolate	¾ pt milk
1½ oz sago	2 tablesp single cream
1 oz glacé cherries, chopped	1 tablesp grape brandy

Grate the chocolate coarsely. Lightly butter a 6 or 7-in casserole. Put the chocolate, sago, cherries, milk and cream in the casserole and mix well. Cover tightly, and cook at not more than 100 °C, 200 °F, Gas Mark 'warm', for 5–6 hr or overnight. Cool.

When cold, stir the brandy into the cream, and transfer to individual coupé glasses.

Decorate with whipped cream and cherries if you wish.

4 helpings

DANISH APPLE PUDDING

8 oz butter	1 teasp crystallized ginger, chopped
8 oz castor sugar	
8 oz self-raising flour	
2 large eggs	1½ lb cooking apples, peeled, cored and dipped in lemon juice
4 oz seedless raisins *or* sultanas	
4 oz soft brown sugar	
2 oz walnuts, shelled and chopped	

Melt the margarine in a flameproof casserole. Remove from the heat; whisk the eggs slightly in a basin with the sugar, and add to the fat. Sift in the flour, and stir to blend. Remove about ¼ of the mixture to a small basin.

Slice the apples thinly and lay neatly on the pudding mixture. Sprinkle on the dried fruit and brown sugar, then the chopped nuts and ginger. Top with spoonfuls of the reserved pudding mixture.

Bake the pudding at 180 °C, 350 °F, Gas Mark 4 for 40–45 min.

6 helpings

HONEYCOMB LEMON PUDDING

6 oz castor sugar	1 dessertsp fresh lemon rind
3 dessertsp flour	
Pinch of salt	2 eggs, separated
Pinch of salt	1½ gills milk
3 dessertsp fresh lemon juice	1 tablesp single cream

Mix the sugar, sifted flour, salt, lemon juice and rind, slightly-beaten egg yolks and milk. Place in the top of a double boiler over simmering water, and stir until the mixture thickens. Remove from the heat, and cool somewhat.

Beat the egg whites until stiff, and fold all but 2 tablesp into the pudding mixture. Pour into a casserole, and stand it in a pan of hot water. Spread the remaining egg white on top. Bake uncovered at 150 °C, 300 °F, Gas Mark 1 for 1 hr. The top and bottom of the pudding will separate as in a honeycomb mould.

4 helpings

PEARS BAKED WITH RED WINE

6 hard cooking pears	About ¼ bottle red wine
3 oz castor sugar per lb of pears	

Peel the pears but do not core them. Leave the stalks on, but cut a small slice from the rounded end of each so that the fruit stands upright. Stand the pears in a heavy tall casserole, which they almost fill. Sprinkle with the sugar. Pour the wine round, and add enough water barely to cover the fruit. Cover, and bake at the lowest possible heat overnight. Leave to cool.

When cold transfer the fruit and juice to a sparklingly clear glass serving bowl, preferably stemmed, and pour the sauce round them. Serve with chilled whipped cream.

6 helpings

CASSEROLE-BAKED CLASSIC RICE PUDDING

2 oz pudding rice	**½ teasp grated**
1 pt milk	**nutmeg or**
2 dessertsp castor	**lemon or**
sugar	**orange rind**
1–2 dessertsp	
shredded suet	

Grease a casserole with a lid, using butter. Put in the rice, and add the milk and sugar. Scatter the suet and the flavouring on top. Cover the casserole, and stand it in a baking tray of hot water. Bake slowly at not more than 150 °C, 300 °F, Gas Mark 1 for 4–5 hours or overnight. ½ hr before turning off the oven, remove the lid of the casserole.

You can vary the amount of milk to give you the consistency you like. Some people like a fairly solid rice pudding, others prefer it to flow over the plate when cooked.

QUEEN'S PUDDING

¼ lb biscuit or	**6–9 apricot**
cake crumbs	**halves, canned**
1 pt milk	*or* **bottled**
2 oz sugar	**Glacé cherries**
2 eggs	
Vanilla essence	

Apricot sauce:

½ pt apricot syrup	**1 tablesp kirsch**
Sugar to taste	*or* **rum**

Rub the crumbs through a fine sieve. Heat the milk, add the crumbs, leave to stand for 10–15 min until soft, then beat until smooth. Beat in the sugar and eggs. Flavour with the essence. Grease a casserole with butter, line the base with a round of greased paper and sprinkle with castor sugar. Pour in the mixture and cover with paper and a lid. Stand the mould in a tin of hot water, and bake in a warm oven (170 °C, 335 °F, Gas 3) until the mixture is firm; this takes about 1 hr.

While the pudding cooks, make the sauce by boiling the apricot syrup with sugar added to taste until it is slightly reduced. Use the syrup from the can or bottle for this. Add the kirsch or rum after reducing it.

When the pudding is set in the middle, leave it to stand for a few minutes, then carefully unmould on to a dish. Tear off the paper, arrange the apricot halves round the dish, decorate the pudding with the cherries and pour the apricot sauce round it.

6 helpings

RASPBERRY PUDDING

1 lb raspberries	**2 eggs**
3 oz granulated	**6 oz plain flour**
sugar	**1 rounded teasp**
4 oz butter *or*	**baking-powder**
margarine	**2–4 tablesp milk**
4 oz castor sugar	**(approx.)**

Grease a shallow casserole. But the cleaned and washed raspberries, with the granulated sugar, in the bottom of the dish.

Cream together in a mixing bowl the butter and castor sugar. Beat in the eggs gradually. Stir in the sifted flour and baking-powder, adding milk to make an easy dropping consistency. Spread this mixture over the fruit. Bake at 180 °C, 350 °F, Gas 4 until the pudding is cooked and nicely browned—about 1–1¼ hr.

Well dredge with castor sugar before serving.

Serve with cream.

6 helpings

SPICED FRUIT PURÉES *(Cont. p. 100)*

Casserole-cooked fruit purées contain all the goodness and flavour of the fruit, and are never mushy. You can use hard cooking fruit or windfalls.

For spice, use ground cloves with apples, ground cinnamon with dates or pears, bay leaves with apricots or peaches. Grated nutmeg also goes well with apples, and mixed spice is good with cherries or damsons.

The amount of flavouring and sweetening will depend on the acidity and flavour of the fruit. Dessert apples usually need no sugar at all when cooked by this method, but pears and tart plums usually need a little.

Chop the fruit roughly after washing it. Do not remove skins or pips, but crack large stones. Place the chopped fruit in a casserole. Add a little water to cover the bottom of the casserole, if the fruit is very hard and dry; soft fruit should not need any.

Seal the casserole tightly, and cook in the oven at 140 °C, 275 °F, Gas Mark ½ overnight. Leave to cool.

When cool, remove any large hard pieces of stone, stalk, etc. Sieve the fruit, skins and all.

Use for fruit fools, bavarian creams, ice-creams and soufflés.

Toppings and Companions for Casseroles

You CAN VARY even the most everyday casseroles with different 'toppings' and trimmings. This section gives you a selection of them, and also some suggestions for side dishes.

In the next section, you will find recipes for the savoury sauces used in earlier recipes in the book and some extra ones.

BACON CURL TOPPINGS

Gently fry or grill thin rinded bacon rashers until almost cooked but still flexible. Stick a fork into one end of a rasher and turn it to curl the rasher into a roll. Place the curls, cut side down, on top of the hot casserole about 5 min before the end of the cooking time. Do not re-cover the casserole.

DUMPLINGS AS TOPPING

3–4 oz suet	1 teasp baking
8 oz flour	powder
¼ teasp salt	Cold water

Make a dough like suet crust pastry. Form into small balls, and leave to firm up before use. Chill if possible. Drop on top of a hot casserole 15–20 min before the end of the cooking time. Re-cover the casserole.

Alternatively drop the dumplings into boiling stock, and simmer for 15–20 minutes. Drain and place on the cooked casserole just before serving.

SAVOURY CHEESE TOPPING

2–4 tablesp grated	2–4 tablesp
cheese	buttered
(see recipe)	breadcrumbs

Mix the grated cheese and crumbs. For the cheese, use equal quantities of Gruyère and Emmentaler, or mature cheddar or firm Lancashire cheese.

Either sprinkle the topping on the hot casserole 5 min before the end of the cooking time, and leave uncovered; or sprinkle on the cooked casserole and place under a moderate grill flame for 2–3 min to brown the top slightly.

SAVOURY CHEESE CRUMBLE TOPPING

5 oz plain flour	Salt
2½ oz margarine	Pinch of dry
2 oz grated	English mustard
Cheddar cheese	Pinch of paprika

Rub or cut the fat into the flour until the mixture resembles fine breadcrumbs. Sprinkle in the remaining ingredients, and blend lightly with a fork.

Sprinkle the crumble over the hot casserole 10–15 min before the end of the cooking time. Do not re-cover the casserole.

SAVOURY CUSTARD TOPPING

2 eggs, slightly	¼ pt single cream
beaten	Salt and pepper

Whisk the eggs and cream together in a basin, and season to suit your taste. Pour on top of the hot cassrole 7–10 min before the end of the cooking time. Do not re-cover the casserole.

Variations

Curry custard Add ½ teasp curry powder with the salt and pepper.

Tomato custard Add 1–2 teasp tomato ketchup to the cream.

SCONE TOPPING

4 oz sifted flour	2 tablesp lard *or*
1½ teasp baking	margarine
powder	Scant ¼ pt milk
¼ teasp salt	

Sift all the dry ingredients together. Cut in the fat with two knives until it resembles coarse breadcrumbs. Add enough milk to moisten, and mix lightly to a firm dough. Pat or roll out the dough to about ½-in thickness. Cut out in rounds or crescents, and drop in a circle round the edge of the *hot* casserole, 10 min before the end of cooking time. Do not cover the casserole again.

Variations

Pimento scones Add 2 tablesp finely-chopped green or red bell pepper to the dry ingredients.

Tangy scones Add 1 tablesp finely-chopped gherkins and ½ teasp dry mustard to the dry ingredients.

SWEET CRUMBLE TOPPING

6 oz plain flour	½ teasp ground
3 oz butter or	ginger *or*
margarine	cinnamon
3 oz castor sugar	(optional)

Sift the flour, and rub in the fat until the mixture resembles fine breadcrumbs. Stir in the sugar and spice lightly. Sprinkle the crumble over any stewed fruit mixture and pat down lightly with the back of a spoon. Bake at 180 °C, 350 °F, Gas Mark 4, for about ½ hr until the crumble is golden.

Dredge with a little extra castor sugar before serving.

Variation

Quick Creamy Crumble Use 1½ oz castor sugar and 1½ oz dried skim milk powder instead of all sugar.

SWEET OATFLAKE CRUNCHIE TOPPING

3 oz plain flour	2 oz Demerara
3 oz rolled oats	sugar
3 oz margarine	

Use this topping for casserole-baked fruit dishes.

Rub the fat into the flour and oats mixed together. Add the sugar. Sprinkle over any casserole of prepared fruit before cooking, and bake in a moderate oven, at about 180 °C, 350 °F, Gas Mark 4, for 30–35 min until both fruit and topping are cooked through.

4–5 helpings

'INSTANT' TOPPINGS

The following toppings are little or no trouble to prepare.

GOLDEN POTATO TOPPING

2–3 cooked	Butter, melted
potatoes	

Slice the potatoes neatly. Brush with melted

butter. Arrange in a circle round the edge of the hot casserole about 15–20 min before the end of the cooking time. Do not re-cover.

POTATO FLUFF TOPPING

4–5 medium sized cooked potatoes or 1 large pkt instant mashed potato	Scant ¼ pt milk 1 egg, slightly beaten

Mash cooked potatoes or prepare instant mashed potato as directed. Make up with rather less milk than usual. Stir in the egg and blend thoroughly. Drop in spoonfuls on the hot casserole 7–8 min before the end of the cooking time. Do not re-cover.

APPLE AND PEPPER TOPPING

1–2 cooking apples, cored but not peeled 1 green bell pepper, cut in rings	Melted butter

Slice the apples horizontally. Brush with melted butter at once. Arrange on top of the casserole with a ring of bell pepper surrounding each one, 10 min before the end of the cooking time. Do not re-cover the casserole.

INSTANT CHEESE TOPPING

Cut thin slices of mild or processed cheese from a square block. Cut into triangles or wedge shapes. Brush lightly with softened or melted butter. Arrange in a pattern on the hot casserole 2–3 min before the end of the cooking time. Do not re-cover the casserole.

TOAST BONNET TOPPING

Spread hot toast with butter or margarine. For extra flavour, sprinkle on a little garlic or onion salt. Cut in small cubes, and scatter on a hot casserole just before serving.

Alternatively cut the toast into small rounds with a biscuit cutter, and arrange in an overlapping circle round the edge of the casserole.

CORNFLAKE TOPPING FOR DESSERTS

2 oz cornflakes 1 level tablesp golden syrup	1 oz butter

Crush the cornflakes slightly. Heat the golden syrup and butter together gently until melted. Stir in the cornflakes. While still warm, spread on a cooked sweet casserole, or a cold dessert (not ice-cream). Leave to 'set'.

QUICK CHOCOLATE TOPPING

Coarsely grated plain or bitter-sweet chocolate makes a good topping for many cold desserts. A mixture of bitter-sweet and milk chocolate also looks and tastes attractive. Fork on loosely.

BABY MERINGUE SHELL TOPPING

Small meringue shells look delightful on individual desserts.

MERINGUE TOPPING AND SHELLS

4 eggs	½ lb castor sugar

Make sure that the egg whites are fresh and contain no trace of yolk or grease. Break down with a whisk to an even-textured liquid by tapping lightly for a few moments. Then whisk evenly and continuously until a firm, stiff, close-textured foam is obtained. Whisk in 1 tablesp of the sugar. Add the rest of the sugar, a little at a time, by folding it in lightly with a metal spoon. For small meringue shells, force through a ⅜-in pipe into small rounds, *or* form into egg-shapes with two spoons, dipped in cold water, and place on strips of oiled kitchen paper on baking sheets. Dredge well with castor sugar and dry in a cool oven (140 °C, 290 °F, Gas 1), placed low to avoid discolouring and reduce to 130 °C, 265 °F,

Gas ½, after 1 hr. If a pure white meringue is required, *very* slow drying is essential, by leaving the meringue in a barely warm oven overnight.

TRIMMINGS AND COMPANIONS

BREADCRUMBS, HOME-MADE

Fresh white breadcrumbs Remove the crusts from some bread that is at least 1 day old and either rub the bread through a fine wire sieve, or grate it; or rub between the palms of the hand until fine crumbs are obtained; the crusts are not used. NOTE: Fresh crumbs will not keep.

Dried white breadcrumbs are fresh white breadcrumbs which have been dried slowly. They may be dried in a very cool oven, or left in a warm place until thoroughly dry. They will keep for several weeks if kept in an airtight tin or jar.

Any crumbs left over from egging and crumbing should be dried in the oven, passed through a sieve, and kept in an airtight tin or jar for future use.

Browned breadcrumbs or raspings Put the crusts or any pieces of stale bread in a moderate oven 180 °C, 350 °F, Gas 4 and bake them until golden and crisp. Then crush them with a rolling-pin or put them through the mincer. Store in an airtight tin or jar. Use for coating croquettes, fish cakes, rissoles, or for covering au gratin dishes.

Fried Breadcrumbs Put some fresh, fine white breadcrumbs in a frying-pan or baking-tin, with a little butter; season with salt and pepper, and either fry or bake until well browned and crisp.

CROÛTES AND CROÛTONS

A croûte is a fried or toasted slice of bread (round square, etc.) often used as a base, usually for a savoury item such as a roast

top Scone Topping

centre Golden potato topping

bottom Apple and pepper topping

Potatoes baked in their jackets

game bird or a meat mixture. Many hors d'œuvres and snacks are served on small round croûtes or fingers of bread. Croûtes are also used as a garnish for a rich dish such as a salmi, or for a hearty casserole, their crispness contrasting with the sauce. Croûtes should be cut from bread at least one day old, and should be $\frac{1}{4}$–$\frac{1}{2}$-in thick.

TO MAKE CRESCENTS OR FLEURONS
Cut bread slices (or pastry) into circles with a pastry cutter. Then cut crescent moon shapes from these, with the same or a slightly smaller cutter.

TO FRY CROÛTES
Use clarified butter or oil, and make sure that the first side is crisp and golden before turning.

TO MAKE TOASTED CROÛTES
Toast whole bread slices, and cut to shape after toasting, using a sharp knife or scissors.

TO MAKE CROÛTONS
Croûtons are small squares or dice of fried or toasted bread usually served with soups. Cut the crusts off $\frac{1}{4}$–$\frac{1}{2}$-in slices of day-old bread, cut into dice and fry until golden on all sides. Alternatively, bake until golden.

HERB FORCEMEAT OR FORCEMEAT BALLS

4 oz breadcrumbs	Nutmeg
2 oz chopped suet *or* margarine	Grated rind of ½ lemon
1 tablesp chopped parsley	Salt and pepper
½ teasp chopped mixed herbs	1 beaten egg

Mix all the ingredients well together, using the egg to form a stiff paste. If liked, roll into balls and fry in deep or shallow fat until golden-brown all over.

PARSLEY AS TRIMMING

Parsley is perhaps the commonest trimming or garnish for all kinds of savoury dishes.

To blanch Bring a saucepan of water to the boil. Place the washed parsley sprigs in a strainer, dip it in the boiling water for a moment, then withdraw it and shake the parsley to dry it.

To Chop Blanch the parsley so that it keeps its greenness and Vitamin C. Wring it in a cloth to dry it. Cut off the stalks, and chop finely with a sharp knife, using a downward, not a 'sawing' stroke. Blanched parsley will not stain the chopping board.

To fry Immerse the washed and dried parsley in deep, hot fat for a few moments only. You can fry the sprigs only, in a strainer, or tie the stalks together with string, leaving a dangling loop by which to hold the parsley while dipping it in the hot fat.

VEGETABLES AS TRIMMINGS

Celery Curls Cut celery in 2-in lengths. Shred lengthwise over a coarse grater. Put shreds into iced water and leave for ½ hr.

Gherkin Fans Make about 6 cuts from the top almost to the base of the gherkins. Spread into fan shapes.

Radish Roses Cut off the roots of the radishes. Make 4–6 cuts in each, almost to the base. Put into iced water; they will open like roses.

Tomato Slices and Lilies Slice unskinned tomatoes with a sharp knife. To make lilies, use a stainless steel knife to make zigzag cuts all round the tomato, into the centre. Pull the 2 halves apart. To skin tomatoes, drop into hot water for a moment. The skins should peel off easily.

LEMON OR ORANGE BASKETS

Take a clean lemon or orange and with a sharp stainless steel knife remove almost a whole quarter segment. Leaving a strip of rind wide enough for the handle, remove the corresponding segment. Remove the pulp from the lower half.

LEMON BUTTERFLIES

Wash and dry a lemon. Cut thin slices from the widest part of the lemon and remove the pips. Cut the slices either in halves or quarters, depending on the width of 'wings' required. Cut through the rind in the middle of each piece and gently pull into 2 wings without breaking into 2 pieces. A piece of parsley may be placed in the centre to represent the butterfly's body.

POTATOES BAKED IN THEIR JACKETS

6 large potatoes	Butter *or* margarine *or* bacon fat

Scrub the potatoes, rinse and dry them. Brush with melted butter, or margarine or bacon fat or rub with a greasy butter paper. Prick with a fork. Bake on the shelves of a fairly hot oven (190 °C, 350 °F, Gas 5) until soft—about 1½ hr. Turn once whilst they are cooking. Make a cut in the top of each, insert a pat of butter or margarine. Serve in a hot vegetable dish.

New potatoes can be cooked in the same way.

6 helpings

ROAST POTATOES

2 lb even-sized potatoes	Salt and pepper Dripping

Peel the potatoes and cut in halves or even

in quarters if very large. Parboil and strain off the water and dry the potatoes over a low heat. Put into hot dripping in a roasting-tin. Roll the potatoes in the fat and cook till tender and brown.

Cooking time, to parboil, 10 min; to bake, 1 hr (approx.)

BRAISED CELERY

4 heads of celery	**Meat glaze (if**
Stock, meat *or*	**available)**
vegetable	
Mirepoix:	
½ oz dripping	**Bouquet garni**
½ oz bacon	**(thyme,**
2 large carrots	**marjoram,**
1 small turnip	**sage, parsley)**
2 onions	**1 bay leaf**
A pinch of mace	**Watercress to**
6 white	**garnish**
peppercorns	**Salt**

Trim the celery but leave the heads whole. Wash them well and tie each securely. Prepare the mirepoix. Fry the bacon in the dripping in a large saucepan, then fry all the vegetables cut in pieces ¾ in thick, until lightly browned. Add herbs, spices and ½ teasp of salt and enough stock to come ¾ of the way up the vegetables. Bring to boiling-point. Lay the celery on top. Baste well with the stock in the pan and cover closely with greased paper or metal foil. Put on lid and cook until the celery is soft (about 1½ hr). Baste several times during cooking. Dish the celery and keep hot. Strain the liquor, put it back in the pan. Reduce by boiling quickly until of glazing consistency or use meat glaze. Pour over the celery. If you wish, place the dish under a hot grill for a moment until it begins to brown. Garnish with watercress.

BRAISED LEEKS

12 leeks	**Mirepoix as for**
Salt	**braised celery**

Trim off the roots and outer leaves and as much of the tops as necessary. Split from the top to within 1 in of the bottom. Wash very thoroughly under running water, separating each leaf with the fingers to ensure that no grit is left between the leaves. Drain and tie in bundles. Parboil in as little water as possible (barely enough to cover), with 1 teasp salt to 1 pt water.

Then follow the same method as for Braised Celery.

6 helpings

STUFFED PEPPERS

6 small *or* **3 large**	**A little melted**
peppers	**butter** *or*
1 tablesp	**margarine**
breadcrumbs	**(optional)**
(optional)	
Stuffing:	
1 oz butter	**1 large cooking**
1 oz flour	**apple, peeled,**
½ pt milk,	**cored and**
warmed	**chopped**
Salt and freshly	**¼ lb grated**
ground black	**Gruyère**
pepper	**cheese**
1 green pepper,	
de-seeded and	
finely chopped	

Wash and parboil the peppers. Drain, cut in half lengthways and remove seeds. Prepare the stuffing. Melt the butter, and add the flour. Cook gently for a few minutes. Add the milk slowly, and season to taste. Cook for a further 2–3 min until sauce thickens slightly. Add the apple, chopped pepper and cheese, and re-season if required. Fill the halved peppers with the stuffing, sprinkle with a few breadcrumbs and a little melted fat if desired. Put the stuffed peppers in a greased shallow casserole, and bake for 30 min at 150 °C, 300 °F, Gas 1–2.

6 helpings

BOILED LONG-GRAIN RICE

8 oz long-grain	**Water to cover**
rice	**1 teasp salt**

Put rice, water and salt into a saucepan, bring to the boil and stir once. Lower heat so that the water only simmers. Cover and cook for about 15 min, or until the water is absorbed.

Braised celery

Alternatively:

½ lb long-grain rice	1 teasp salt
2 oz butter	¼ teasp pepper
1 small onion, finely chopped	Stock
½ teasp saffron	1 pt tomato sauce
Nutmeg	2 oz grated Parmesan cheese

Wash, drain and dry the rice thoroughly in a clean cloth. Heat the butter in a saucepan, put in the onion, and when lightly browned add the rice, and shake the pan over the heat for about 10 min. Then sprinkle in the saffron, a good pinch of nutmeg, salt and pepper. Cover with stock, and cook gently for about 1 hr adding meanwhile the tomato sauce and as much stock as the rice will absorb, the sauce being added when the rice is about half cooked. Just before serving stir in the cheese.

This savoury rice is frequently used for borders instead of plainly boiled rice or mashed potatoes.

Either of these recipes can be used as a main dish, accompanied by small bowls of chutney, cooked shrimps, shredded green peppers or canned red pimentos, sliced hard-boiled eggs and other hors d'oeuvre or salad ingredients. Each person can then choose which garnishes he prefers.

2–3 helpings

To serve hot, rinse the rice under hot water and top with a few flakes of butter if desired. If wanted for a salad, rinse under cold water, cool, cover and chill.

RISOTTO

4 oz long-grain rice	1 pt vegetable stock *or* water
1 small onion	Salt and pepper
2 oz butter	2 tablesp grated Parmesan cheese

Wash and dry the rice thoroughly. Chop the onion finely; heat the butter and fry the onion until lightly browned. Then add the rice and fry it until brown. Put in the stock or water, add salt and pepper to taste, boil rapidly for 10 min and afterwards simmer slowly until the rice has absorbed all the liquid. Stir in the cheese, add more seasoning if necessary, then serve.

BAKED TOMATOES

6 tomatoes	Finely chopped tarragon (optional)
A little butter *or* margarine	
Salt and pepper	Browned breadcrumbs (optional)
Castor sugar	

Wash the tomatoes and cut them in halves. Put them in a greased, deep fireproof dish. Season and sprinkle each with a pinch of sugar and a pinch of chopped tarragon, if used. Put a tiny piece of butter on each or cover with a well greased paper. Bake in a moderate oven (180 °C, 350 °F, Gas 4) until soft—about 20 min.

Stuffed peppers

Alternatively, cut the tomatoes in half
horizontally or make crossways cuts in the
top of each. Press the cut portion into
browned breadcrumbs before baking and
top with the butter or margarine.

6 helpings

Sauces you will need for Fondues and Bakes

AGRO-DOLCE

1 onion	¼ pt red wine
1 carrot	⅛ pt wine vinegar
1 clove of garlic	2 oz sugar
(optional)	2 tablesp water
1 bay leaf	¼ pt good meat
6 peppercorns	gravy
1 tablesp olive oil	

Sweetening:

Any one or any mixture of the following to taste: 1 teasp chopped mint; 1 teasp finely-shredded candied orange peel; 1 dessertsp chopped nuts; 1 dessertsp sultanas; 1 tablesp grated bitter chocolate

Chop the onion and carrot, crush the garlic. Cook them with the bay leaf and peppercorns very gently in the oil for 15–20 min. Drain off the oil and add the wine and vinegar. Simmer gently ½ hr. In a separate pan boil the sugar, dissolved in the water until it turns golden brown. Add to this the wine mixture. Add the gravy and any one or any mixture of the sweetening ingredients to taste.

ANCHOVY SAUCE

To ½ pt basic white sauce made from fish stock *or* water *or* ½ milk and ½ water add 1 *or* 2 teasp anchovy essence to taste and a few drops lemon juice and a few drops of cochineal to tint the sauce a dull pink.

BASIC BROWN SAUCE

1 small carrot	1 oz flour
1 onion	1 pt brown stock
1 oz dripping	Salt and pepper

Thinly slice the carrot and onion. Melt the dripping and in it slowly fry the onion and carrot until they are golden-brown. Stir in the flour and fry it even more slowly till it is also golden-brown. Stir in the stock, bring to simmering point, season, then simmer for ½ hr. Strain the sauce before use. As the frying of the flour is a long process, extra colour may be given to the sauce by adding a piece of brown onion skin, or a little gravy browning or a little meat or vegetable extract which will also add to the flavour.

Cooking time 40 min–1 hr

BASIC WHITE SAUCE

2 oz butter *or*	1 pt milk *or* stock
margarine	(fish, meat *or*
2 oz flour	vegetable to
Pinch of salt	suit dish), *or* a
	mixture of
	stock and milk

Melt the fat in a deep saucepan, large

enough to hold the amount of liquid with just enough room to spare for beating the sauce. Stir the flour into the fat and allow it to bubble for 2–3 min over a gentle heat. On no account allow it to change colour; this is a white roux. Remove from heat and stir in ½ the liquid gradually. Return to moderate heat and stir the sauce briskly until it thickens, then beat it vigorously. Season and use.

A coating sauce should coat the back of the wooden spoon used for stirring, and should only just settle to its own level in the pan.

Cooking time 15 min

Variations:

To ½ pt basic white sauce made with stock, or ½ milk and ½ stock, add, just before serving:

Caper sauce 1 tablesp capers and 1 teasp vinegar from caper pickle.

Cucumber sauce ¼ medium cucumber, diced.

Horseradish sauce 1 rounded tablesp grated horseradish, 1 teasp vinegar and ½ teasp sugar.

Maître d'Hôtel sauce Juice of ½ lemon, 1 rounded tablesp finely-chopped parsley and 1 oz extra butter.

Parsley sauce 1 tablesp finely-chopped parsley and 1 oz extra butter.

BEARNAISE SAUCE

¼ pt Béchamel sauce	2–3 egg yolks
2 shallots	4 oz butter
Sprig of tarragon	2 teasp lemon
Sprig of chervil	juice
6 peppercorns	Salt and pepper
⅛ pt white wine *or* wine vinegar	

Chop shallots and herbs. Put wine in a very small pan with the shallots, herbs and peppercorns and simmer gently till reduced by ½, then strain. Mix egg yolks and sauce and heat them in a double boiler or in a basin over a pan of hot water. Add the wine and whisk in the butter, a pat at a time, until all is absorbed. The water must

not be allowed to boil or the sauce will curdle. Season sauce and add lemon juice, add a little chopped tarragon and chervil and use sauce at once.

BÉCHAMEL SAUCE

1 pt milk	6 peppercorns
1 small onion	A small bunch of
1 small carrot	herbs
2 in celery stick	2 oz butter
1 bay leaf	2 oz flour
1 clove	⅛ pt cream
¼ teasp mace	(optional)
Salt	

Warm the milk with the vegetables, herbs, salt and spices, and bring it slowly to simmering point. Put a lid on the pan and stand it in a warm place on the cooker to infuse for ½ hr. Strain the milk, melt the butter, add the flour. Cook this roux for a few minutes without browning it. Stir the flavoured milk gradually into the roux. Bring the sauce to boiling point, stirring vigorously. If cream is used, add it to the sauce just at boiling point and do not reboil it.

CRANBERRY SAUCE

½ lb cranberries	Sugar to taste
¼–½ pt water	

Stew the cranberries till soft, using ¼ pt water and adding more if needed. Rub the fruit through a hair or nylon sieve. Sweeten to taste. For economy, half cranberries and half sour cooking apples make an excellent sauce. Serve with roast turkey, chicken *or* game.

CREAM SALAD DRESSING (1)

½ level teasp mixed English mustard *or* French mustard	4 tablesp double cream
	1 tablesp vinegar (wine *or* malt with a little tarragon)
1 level saltsp salt	
1 saltsp castor sugar	

Mix the mustard, salt and sugar smoothly

Ingredients for savoury sauces

together. Stir in the cream. Add the vinegar drop by drop, beating mixture all the time.

If you prefer, use only 2 tablesp cream and add 1 tablesp oil. In this case, use only a dessertsp vinegar, and add the oil, drop by drop, to the cream mixture before adding the vinegar.

CREAM SALAD DRESSING (2)

¼ pt thick soured cream *or* 3 oz rich full-fat soft cheese *and* 2 dessertsp milk *and* juice of ½ lemon	Salt and pepper Mixed English mustard *or* French mustard Castor sugar

If using cheese, mix it with the milk and lemon juice until smooth. Flavour the cream or soft cheese mixture with salt, pepper, mustard and sugar. Add a little top of the milk if too thick.

CUMBERLAND SAUCE (COLD)

1 orange	¼ teasp mixed
1 lemon	mustard
⅛ pt water	Salt
⅛ pt port wine	Cayenne pepper
2 tablesp vinegar	6–8 glacé cherries
¼ lb redcurrant jelly	

Grate the rind of the orange and lemon, carefully avoiding the pith. Simmer the rinds in the water for 10 min. Add the wine, vinegar, jelly and mustard and

Basic white sauce on cauliflower

Béchamel sauce

simmer them together until the jelly is completely melted. Add the juice of the orange and lemon, season to taste and cool. Chop the glacé cherries and add them to the sauce.

CREAM SAUCE

½ pt Béchamel sauce	Lemon juice to taste
Cayenne pepper	⅛ pt cream
Salt	

Heat the sauce; add the cayenne, salt and lemon juice. Stir cream into seasoned sauce, just below boiling point. On no account allow sauce to boil or it will curdle. Serve at once.

CREAMED YOGURT DIP

1 (8-oz) carton natural yogurt	1 level teasp paprika
4 oz cream cheese	½–1 level teasp salt
2 level tablesp finely-chopped cucumber	Pinch of white pepper

Beat the yogurt into the cheese. Season to suit your taste, and chill well.

CREOLE SAUCE

½ pt Espagnole sauce	½ red sweet pepper
1 onion	1 oz butter
4 mushrooms	Salt and pepper
1 green sweet pepper	1 tablesp chopped parsley

Finely chop the onion and mushrooms, cut the peppers into fine shreds. Cook them in the butter, very gently, for 10 min. Add the sauce and simmer very gently for 1 hr. Season to taste and add the chopped parsley. Do not strain the sauce.

CURRIED CREAM CHEESE DIP

½ lb cream cheese	2 level teasp finely-grated onion
4 tablesp mayonnaise	
1 (8 oz) carton natural yogurt	Salt
3–4 teasp curry powder	

Beat the cheese with the mayonnaise and yogurt until very smooth. Stir in the curry powder and onion. Season to suit your taste. Chill well before serving.

113

CURRY SAUCE (MILD)

1 medium-sized onion	Salt
1 oz butter or margarine	½ pt pale stock, coconut infusion (see below) or water
1 small cooking apple	½ teasp black treacle
¼–½ oz curry powder	1–2 teasp lemon juice
½ oz rice flour or flour	1 dessertsp chutney

Chop the onion, put it into a saucepan and fry it very gently in the butter for 10 min. Chop the apple and cook it in the butter with the onion for a further 10 min. Stir in the curry powder and heat it for a few minutes. Add the flour and then stir in the liquid. When boiling, add all the other ingredients and simmer the sauce for at least ½ hr, or better for 1½ hr.

To make the coconut infusion soak 1 oz desiccated or fresh grated coconut in ½ pt water for a few minutes, bring slowly to boiling point and infuse it for 10 min. Wring the coconut in a piece of muslin to extract all the liquid.

ESPAGNOLE SAUCE

1 onion	2 oz flour
1 carrot	1 pt brown stock
2 oz mushrooms or mushroom trimmings	Bouquet garni
	6 peppercorns
	1 bay leaf
2 oz lean raw ham or bacon	¼ pt tomato pulp
	Salt
2 oz butter or dripping	⅛ pt sherry (optional)

Slice the vegetables, chop the ham. Melt the fat and fry the ham for a few minutes and then, very slowly, the vegetables until they are golden-brown. Add the flour and continue frying very slowly till all is a rich brown. Add the stock, herbs and spices and stir till the sauce simmers; simmer for ½ hr. Add the tomato pulp and simmer the sauce for a further ½ hr. Wring the sauce through a tammy cloth or rub it through a fine hair or nylon sieve. Season, add the sherry, if used, and re-heat the sauce.

DEVIL SAUCE

1 oz butter, margarine or beef dripping	1 teasp mixed mustard
	¼ teasp pepper
1 oz flour	½ teasp grated lemon rind
½ pt good meat gravy	½ teasp chopped shallot
1–2 tablesp Worcester or other commercial sauce	1 teasp chopped capers
	½ teasp chilli vinegar
2 teasp lemon	A very little cayenne pepper
¼ teasp anchovy essence	

Make a brown sauce with the fat, flour and gravy. Add all the other ingredients to taste and simmer them together for 5–10 minutes.

FRENCH DRESSING

2–3 tablesp olive oil	¼ teasp castor sugar
Pepper and salt	1 tablesp wine vinegar
Pinch of dry English mustard	

Mix the oil and seasoning. Add the vinegar gradually, stirring constantly with a wooden spoon so that an emulsion is formed.

Alternatively, make the sauce in a bottle with a tight stopper. Keep it in the fridge, and shake vigorously before use. French dressing will keep for several days if chilled.

Lemon juice can be used in place of vinegar. Where suitable, orange or grapefruit juice can also be used.

HOLLANDAISE SAUCE

2 tablesp wine vinegar	2–4 oz butter
2 egg yolks	Salt and pepper
	Lemon juice

Boil the vinegar till it is reduced by half; allow to cool. Mix the cool vinegar with the egg yolks in a basin and place this over hot water. Whisk the egg yolks till they begin to thicken, then whisk in the butter gradually until all is absorbed. Season, add lemon juice to taste and serve immediately if possible. If not, stand the container in a larger pan of hot water.

ITALIAN SAUCE

½ pt Espagnole sauce	⅛ pt white wine (optional)
4 shallots	Parsley stalks
6 mushrooms	Sprig of thyme
1 tablesp olive oil	1 bay leaf
⅛ pt stock	Salt and pepper

Chop the shallots and mushrooms and cook them very gently for 10 min in the olive oil. Add the stock, wine (if used), herbs and spices and simmer gently until reduced by half. Add the Espagnole sauce and cook gently for 20 min. Season, and lift out the herbs.

MAYONNAISE

1–2 egg yolks	4 parts wine,
Salt and pepper	vinegar or
Mustard	lemon juice, 2
¼–½ pt best olive oil	parts tarragon and 1 part chilli
Mixed vinegars to taste—if possible,	vinegar

The eggs and oil should be at the same temperature and not too cold. In summer it is easier to make a good mayonnaise beginning with 2 egg yolks.

Remove every trace of egg white from the yolks. Put the yolks in a thick basin which will stand steady in spite of vigorous beating. Add to the egg yolks the pepper, salt and mustard to taste. Drop by drop, add the olive oil, beating or whisking vigorously all the time. As the mayonnaise thickens, the olive oil can be poured in a thin, steady stream but whisking must never slacken. When the mixture is really thick a few drops of vinegar or lemon juice stirred in will thin it again. Continue whisking in the oil, alternately with a little vinegar until the whole amount is added.

If the mayonnaise should curdle, break a fresh egg yolk into a clean basin and beat into this the curdled mixture just as the oil was added originally.

Various other ingredients are often added to mayonnaise, to give a different flavour and colour. They are useful when making a mixed hors d'œuvre or any other dish of mixed products coated with mayonnaise, for they identify the different ingredients, and emphasize their variety.

Some variations are complex sauces in their own right. But it is hardly worth making these for light savoury dishes where, as a rule, only a small amount of each sauce is needed. So the following simple additions to plain Mayonnaise are suggested instead.

To ¼ pt mayonnaise, add:

1 2 tablesp concentrated tomato purée and 1 sweet red pepper, chopped (Andalusian Sauce)

2 1 tablesp cooked spinach purée and 2 tablesp single cream (Green Mousseline Sauce)

3 ½ teasp horseradish cream, 1 teasp each chopped parsley and chervil (Escoffier Sauce)

4 1 tablesp yogurt (or sour cream), ½ teasp chopped chives and a few drops each of Worcester Sauce and lemon juice (Gloucester Sauce)

5 1 oz mixed chopped fresh herbs, as many as you can get (Mayonnaise Verte)

An electric blender makes almost foolproof mayonnaise. Use a whole egg instead of yolks and 2 tablesp vinegar. Put these into the goblet with the seasoning and whisk at high speed for 10 seconds. Still whisking, trickle in the oil gradually. The mixture will start to thicken after ¼ pt has gone in, and will not 'take' more than ½ pt.

White wine can be used instead of wine vinegar, and wine vinegar with a drop or two of Tabasco Sauce can replace the chilli vinegar.

MUSHROOM SAUCE (BROWN)

½ pt basic brown sauce	2–4 oz mushrooms (field if possible)

Italian sauce on kidneys

Chop the mushroom stalks and fry with the other vegetables when making the brown sauce. Add the mushrooms with the stock when making the sauce, and simmer until tender. Strain the sauce, chop the mushrooms and return them to the sauce.

MUSHROOM SAUCE (WHITE)

½ pt basic white   2–4 oz
   sauce   mushrooms
                     ½–1 oz butter

Cook the thinly sliced mushrooms very gently in the butter for 15–20 min. Stir the mushrooms with the butter and their juice into the hot sauce.

OLIVE AND ALMOND SAUCE

5 tablesp butter   4 oz slivered
7 tablesp plain   almonds
   flour   4 oz sliced green
1½ gills single   olives
   cream   1 tablesp lemon
1 teasp salt   juice
1¼ pt chicken   A few grains
   bouillon   cayenne pepper
¼ teasp white
   pepper

Melt the butter in a saucepan, and stir in the flour. Blend until smooth and work in 1 tablesp cream and the salt. Add the chicken bouillon gradually, stirring continuously. When the sauce thickens, stir in

116

Curry sauce and tomato sauce ▶

the rest of the cream, seasonings, almonds, olives and lemon juice. Serve hot.

SAVOURY ORANGE SAUCE

½ pt Espagnole sauce	2 tablesp redcurrant jelly
½ orange	Salt
½ lemon	Cayenne pepper
⅛ pt red wine (optional)	Pinch of sugar

Remove the outer orange rind without the pith, and cut it in neat, thin strips. Cover the orange rind with a little cold water; stew till just tender; then strain. Squeeze the orange and lemon juice into the sauce, add the orange rind. Re-heat, add the wine (if used), the redcurrant jelly, season with salt, pepper and sugar to taste.

ONION SAUCE—WHITE

To ½ pt white sauce made from ½ milk and ½ liquor in which onions were boiled, add 2 chopped, cooked onions and a few drops of lemon juice.

PIQUANT SAUCE

½ pt basic brown sauce	1 tablesp chopped gherkins
1 onion or 2 shallots	1 dessertsp mushroom ketchup
1 oz mushrooms	½ teasp sugar (optional)
1 bay leaf	
¼ teasp mace	
2 tablesp vinegar	
1 tablesp halved capers	

Finely chop the onion or shallots and chop the mushrooms coarsely. Simmer the onion or shallots, the bay leaf and mace in the vinegar for 10 min. Add this mixture and the chopped mushrooms to the brown sauce and simmer till the mushrooms are soft. Add all the other ingredients. Do not strain the sauce but lift out the bay leaf and mace.

This sauce may also be made with an Espagnole foundation.

POIVRADE SAUCE (PEPPER SAUCE)

½ pt Espagnole sauce	½ glass red wine
2 shallots	2 tablesp wine vinegar
1 sprig of thyme	Ground pepper to taste
1 bay leaf	
12 peppercorns	

Finely chop the shallots and simmer them with the herbs and spices in the wine and vinegar until reduced by half. Strain the liquid into the hot Espagnole sauce and add extra ground pepper to taste.

POLONAISE SAUCE

½ pt Velouté sauce	1 teasp finely-chopped fennel
⅛ pt sour cream or yoghourt	1 teasp lemon juice
1 teasp grated horseradish	

Blend all the other ingredients with the hot Velouté sauce. Reheat without boiling.

REFORM SAUCE

½ pt Poivrade sauce	1 dessertsp shredded cooked tongue
½ small glass port	1 dessertsp chopped hard-boiled egg white
1 tablesp redcurrant jelly	
1 dessertsp shredded gherkin	
1 dessertsp chopped, cooked mushrooms	

Gently heat all the ingredients in the Poivrade sauce.

SAVOURY LEMON SAUCE

½ pt white sauce made with chicken or fish stock, or milk and stock	1 tablesp chopped parsley (optional)
1 lemon	½ teasp sugar (optional)
1–2 tablesp cream (optional)	

Peel the rind from the lemon very thinly and simmer it in the milk or stock for 10 min. Strain the liquid and with it make the white sauce. Carefully stir the juice of the lemon and then the cream into the hot sauce but do not boil it again. Sweeten if liked.

SHALLOT SAUCE

6 shallots	½ teasp lemon juice
1 oz butter	Salt and pepper
½ pt good gravy *or* demi-glace sauce	½ teasp finely chopped parsley
1 glass sherry	

Chop the shallots finely, melt the fat in a sauté pan, fry them lightly then drain well. Cool them slightly. To the gravy or demi-glace sauce, add the sherry, lemon juice, well-drained shallots, seasoning and parsley. Boil well until reduced, season to taste and keep hot until needed.

SOUBISE SAUCE

½ pt Béchamel sauce	1–2 tablesp stock
½ lb onions	Salt and pepper
1½ oz butter	Sugar
	Nutmeg

Peel and slice the onions and cook them gently in ½ oz of the butter and just enough stock to moisten them. When they are tender, sieve them or process in an electric blender. Have the sauce very thick, add to it the onion purée, re-heat, season and add sugar and nutmeg to taste. Whisk the remaining 1 oz butter into the sauce at boiling point, adding a small pat at a time. Do not allow the sauce to boil.

SOUR—SWEET SAUCE

2 onions	2 tablesp sugar
1½ oz butter *or* margarine	1 level teasp French mustard
1½ oz flour	1 level teasp Yeast *or* meat extract
¾ pt water *or* stock	Salt and pepper
4 tablesp vinegar	
1–2 teasp any good commercial bottled sauce	

Chop the onions, put into a saucepan and fry them till tender and golden-brown in the butter. Add the flour and brown it a very little. Stir in the liquid, bring to the boil, stirring all the time. Add the other ingredients and simmer the sauce for 15–20 min.

SUPRÊME SAUCE

½ pt Velouté sauce	½–1 oz butter
2 tablesp—⅛ pt cream	Nutmeg to taste
1 egg yolk	Lemon juice
	Salt and pepper

Heat the Velouté sauce, preferably in a double boiler. Mix the egg yolk and cream, and stir into the sauce. Cook without boiling until the egg yolk thickens. Whisk in the butter, a small pat at a time. Add a pinch of nutmeg, a few drops of lemon juice, season and use the sauce at once.

TARTARE SAUCE

¼ pt mayonnaise	A little French mustard
1 teasp each of chopped gherkin, chopped olives, chopped capers, chopped parsley, chopped chives	1 dessertsp wine vinegar
	A little dry white wine (optional)

Mix the chopped ingredients into the mayonnaise, add the mustard. Thin to the required consistency with the vinegar and wine. Use this sauce for light, cold fish and meat first courses as well as hors d'œuvres.

TARTARE SAUCE, QUICK
(Method, p. 120)

1 4-oz can cream	1 tablesp white vinegar
2 tablesp chopped capers	¼ pt bottled *or* home-made mayonnaise (optional)
2 tablesp chopped gherkins	
1 tablesp lemon juice	
1 dessertsp castor sugar	

Chill the cream. When cold, open the can, and pour off the whey. Mix with the other ingredients in a bowl. Chill for an hour before use.

TOMATO SAUCE

1 onion	$\frac{1}{2}$ oz cornflour
1 small carrot	$\frac{1}{2}$ pt white stock
1 oz bacon scraps	or liquid from
or bacon bone or	canned or
rinds	bottled
$\frac{1}{2}$ oz butter or	tomatoes
margarine	Salt and pepper
4 medium-sized	Lemon juice
tomatoes,	Sugar
fresh, bottled	Grated nutmeg
or canned	

Slice the onion and carrot. Put them into a saucepan with the bacon and fry them in the fat without browning them for 10 min. Slice and add the tomatoes and cook them for 5 min. Sprinkle in the corn flour, add the stock or juice, stir till the sauce boils. Simmer the sauce for 45 min. Rub the sauce through a hair or nylon sieve. Reheat, season and add lemon juice, sugar and nutmeg to taste.

VELOUTÉ SAUCE

2 oz butter	2 oz flour
6 button	1 pt good
mushrooms or	vegetable stock
mushroom	(see above)
trimmings	Salt and pepper
12 peppercorns	Lemon juice
A few parsley	$\frac{1}{8}$–$\frac{1}{4}$ pt cream
stalks	

Melt the butter in a saucepan and gently cook the mushrooms, peppercorns and parsley for 10 min. Add the flour and cook for a few minutes without browning it. Stir in the stock, bring the sauce to simmering point and simmer for 1 hr. Wring the sauce through a tammy cloth or damp muslin. Season, add lemon juice, and reheat. Just at boiling point stir in the cream. The mushrooms may be rinsed and used as garnish for the dish.

For fish dishes, use fish stock.

VINAIGRETTE SAUCE

This consists of a simple French dressing to which the following are added:

1 teasp finely-chopped gherkin
$\frac{1}{2}$ teasp finely-chopped shallot or chives
$\frac{1}{2}$ teasp finely-chopped parsley
1 teasp finely-chopped capers
$\frac{1}{2}$ teasp finely-chopped tarragon and chervil (if available)

WHITE ITALIAN SAUCE

$\frac{1}{2}$ pt Béchamel	Salt and pepper
sauce	Lemon juice to
2 shallots	taste
2 oz button	1 dessertsp
mushrooms	chopped
$\frac{1}{2}$ oz butter	parsley ·
$\frac{1}{4}$ pt fish or	2 tablesp cream
vegetable stock	
$\frac{1}{2}$ glass dry white	
wine (optional)	

Chop the shallots and mushrooms very fine. Melt the butter and in it cook the mushrooms and shallots

WHITE WINE SAUCE

$\frac{1}{2}$ pt white stock	$\frac{1}{8}$ pt white wine
or fish stock	1–2 egg yolks
2 oz butter	Juice of $\frac{1}{2}$ lemon
1 oz flour	Salt and pepper

Make a white sauce with the stock, $\frac{1}{2}$ the butter and the flour. Add the wine to this and simmer it for 10 min. Whisk in the remaining butter just below boiling point, then stir in the egg yolks mixed with lemon juice; season. Thicken the egg yolks without letting the sauce boil again.

CIDER SAUCE

$\frac{1}{2}$ pt brown sauce	$\frac{1}{2}$ clove
$\frac{1}{4}$ pt cider	Salt and pepper
$\frac{1}{2}$ bay leaf	

Mix all the ingredients and simmer the sauce to reduce it to the required thickness. Strain the sauce.

Supréme sauce on a chicken dish

Some menus for Casserole-Baked Meals

1
Beef à la Mode
Lettuce Salad
Queen's Pudding
Coffee

2
Beef Olives
Brussels Sprouts Salad
Danish Apple Pudding
Tea

3
Estouffade of Beef
Grissini or Bread Sticks
Tomato and Onion Salad or Crudités
Caramel Rice Pudding
Coffee

4
Midsummer Lamb Casserole
Parker House Rolls
Cauliflower
Spiced fresh fruit purée
   served cold with cream
Milk

5
Braised chilled lamb with Paprika
Boiled rice
Beetroot Salad
Raspberry Pudding
Yogurt

6
Golden Harvest Chicken Casserole
Endive Salad
Apricot and Nut Casserole
Coffee

7
Potato and Bacon Casserole
Carrot Salad
Honeycomb Lemon Pudding
Tea

8
(For a dinner party)
Melon Salad
Casserole of Shellfish with Rice
Coffee and Brandy Cream
   with Mocha Biscuits
Coffee

Index